BARTER SYSTEMS

A NEW WAY TO OFFSET START-UP
EXPENSES, REDUCE INVENTORIES,
CONSERVE CASH FLOW, AND
OPEN NEW MARKETS

BARTER SYSTEMS

A BUSINESS GUIDE FOR TRADE EXCHANGES

ROGER LANGRICK

LONGMEADOW
PRESS

Published by Longmeadow Press,
201 High Ridge Road, Stamford, CT 06904.

Cover design by Kelvin P. Oden
Interior design by Donna R. Miller

Langrick, Roger.
    Barter systems / Roger Langrick. — 1st ed.
        p.   cm.
    Includes index.
    ISBN 0-681-45230-7
    1. Barter—United States. 2. Countertrade—United States.
I. Title.
HF1019.L36   1994
380.1—dc20
                                                93-40405
                                                CIP

Printed in United States of America
First Edition
2 4 6 8 9 7 5 3 1

Contents

Introduction:
Barter, the New Marketplace

Getting America back to work, recovering our place in world markets, bringing the American Dream back into focus—how possible is it to fulfill these goals? Social pundits, using statistics and crystal balls, tend to be pessimistic. They talk of readjusting to a harsher economic reality of tightened belts and lowered expectations. They may be right, but there's no reason to assume they are. There is plenty of proof around that Americans still have the ingenuity to reverse a depressed economy and to revive the American Dream.

One example of this ingenuity is already changing the nation's marketplace. It's barter, the innovative business technique that could not only help revitalize our economy at home but could vault American industry back into the forefront of world trade. American entrepreneurs are leading the world in this updated version of an age-old practice, and in the process they are reshaping the way the world does business.

THE SCOPE OF BARTER

Although bartering on a neighborly basis has always been a part of our everyday lives, the new barter is presenting practical solutions to today's most sophisticated business problems. It is already a valued part of America's marketplace, helping in many unsuspected ways. Every day a CEO somewhere breathes a sigh of relief because he has found a profitable outlet for his excess inventory through systemized barter. A machinist at his lathe may not realize it, but his job may depend on management's ability to move his product through barter as well as through conventional sales outlets. A freelance greeting card designer takes her daughter on a long-promised trip to Florida and pays for it all through barter. An executive uses barter to pay for cosmetic surgery after a car accident. Tomorrow a housewife will find a welcome bargain on canned tomatoes, not realizing they were put on the shelf through an international barter agreement.

Barter deals may still be simple one-on-one swaps, but a growing number are made through a *commercial barter system,* an aggressive new way of dealing with economic downturns and a lack of cash. Systemized barter, using high-tech equipment and management techniques, is emerging as one of the major growth industries of the century, helping individuals and corporations increase their bottom line. It's an industry that has left behind the old images of hippies, swap meets, and fast-talking hustlers and is now embraced as much by Fortune 500 companies as it is by small businesses.

From tumultuous beginnings twenty years ago, systemized barter has grown into a sober-minded option for cash-strapped businesses and corporations clogged with excess inventory. And it is showing promise far beyond its original, limited uses. Many industry observers say that systemized barter has the potential to revive the economy and create a new and vibrant marketplace, at home in the United States and internationally.

THE BARTER NETWORK

A modern barter network is a computerized system with hundreds, maybe thousands, of members exchanging services and goods on a regular basis. Does "barter" really mean that all these people are simply swapping with each other? Technically, yes, but in a barter network the need for face-to-face trade has been eliminated. Instead of cash, a barter network uses trade credits to keep track of who owes what. You sell for trade credits and you buy with trade credits: it's that simple. From the client's point of view it's difficult to distinguish a barter deal from a straight business transaction except for the **"T"** in front of the dollar sign. That **T** means they are talking now in "trade dollars," not cash.

How a Trade Credit Works

A trade dollar or credit as used in a barter system is a substitute for cash, and any client within the network accepts the trade credits issued by the network instead of cash. For instance, if you owned a jewelry store and belonged to the XYZ Trade Exchange, you would sell a $100 pendant to another member for one hundred trade credits (written as $T100). The sale is rung through using a plastic identification card issued by the exchange, and the sale is processed in the same manner as any credit card purchase. The purchaser has his/her account debited by the exchange, and you have your account credited with a $T100.

You can now go to any other member of the exchange and purchase $T100 worth of products or services using your own credit card. If you choose a $T100 meal at a member's restaurant, you have effectively traded your pendant for a meal, no cash involved.

Within its own network, a trade credit works precisely the same way as cash. You can borrow trade credits, you can buy with them, and some networks even offer interest on unspent trade credits in your account.

New Rules

Using trade credits instead of cash means the rules of the game are different and need some study. But in spite of a "smoke and mirrors" reputation among the general public, accessing and using the barter marketplace at a local or even international level is no more difficult than signing up for another credit card or entering into a standard business agreement.

Members' Initiatives with Trade Dollars

Members of trade exchanges often show a lot of initiative in using trade credits. When challenged to show how trade credits could be used to reduce an electricity bill, Fred Lewis, an avid barterer in Seattle, immediately rattled off ideas such as buying solar panels, a generator, storm windows, an electric blanket (lower bedroom temperatures), and even retrofitting the house for maximum insulation and minimum heat loss.

All of these products and services were available through a local exchange, Cascade Trading Association, and all could be acquired on 100 percent barter.

WHAT YOU CAN BARTER

Even the smallest barter network has moved a long way from dealing solely in items such as haircuts or used lawnmowers. Today members of the nation's larger exchanges can access products and services such as tires, airline tickets, quality restaurants, real estate, accommodations in motel and hotel chains, home repair items, paint, printing, cooking utensils, trade and professional services . . . the list goes on and on, and it's all barter.

COMMERCIAL BARTER

Most of the larger barter networks cater almost exclusively to companies that use barter to offset business expenses, trade unwanted inventory, and get the competitive edge in a new market. Many barter networks offer their clients literally thousands of products and services that can be bought for trade credits, and some corporations trade up to $100,000 a year. Some even use barter networks as a way of maximizing production time, using slack periods between customized orders to produce extra product for barter. For instance, a custom wrought-iron handrail manufacturer explained that by producing one extra set of rails, he could reduce his initial setup cost, save money for his customer, and trade the extra set through his local network for his own needs.

REDUCED CASH FLOW

People who barter say the need for real money is often a lot less than may be imagined. Because businesses can access through barter many of the supplies they usually pay cash for, using trade credits conserves precious cash flow. Barter industry estimates are that if you own a small business with under a hundred employees, you will save up to 20 percent of your usual monthly cash expenditures by bartering for them instead of paying cash. The total annual trading dollar volume of small businesses accessing their supplies through trade exchanges was over $700 million in 1993.

Each trade dollar can be viewed in two different ways: as a direct saving of cash outlay or as incremental business, additional income that would not have been there without the trade exchange. Some barterers estimate that as many as one out of every five new customers come through their barter network contacts.

Who Joins?

It's hard to define a typical member—or *client,* as most exchanges insist on calling them. Ten years ago a client of America's trade exchanges was most likely to be a small business, usually in the service industry. Today, barter casts a much wider net, and a typical member could be a two-man welding shop grossing $100,000 annually or a manufacturer doing $250 million in sales.

Regardless of the size of their firms, barter exchange clients have certain traits in common. First and foremost they have all mastered the art of seeing their needs in relationship to what they can offer, not simply what they can afford. Most of us adjust our business decisions and expenditures to suit whatever money we have, but in many cases what we really want is not cash but purchasing power. Barterers say that by insisting on going through the sell-save-spend cycle, we discount our *other* purchasing power: our skills, service, or product.

Another quality found in the successful barter is the ability to be innovative. The nature of barter requires different tactics and broader thinking than the cash market. Even the largest barter networks have a restricted supply of goods and services when compared with the open marketplace, and people who join barter systems must be quick in decision making and able to seize a chance or a product when it appears. In the regular marketplace, the emphasis is first on getting the money and second on spending it. In a barter network, the system works best if you first make out your shopping list and then find ways of fulfilling it. This attitude—of putting your own needs first—creates quite a different feeling in the barter economy. Most of us are avid sellers, either of product or service. Barterers, on the other hand, are avid shoppers, always looking for ways to trade what they have for what they want.

In brief, the best type of exchange client is one who has taken the time to understand the benefits of barter, is keen about the process, and wants to use it on an ongoing basis.

CORPORATE TRADE EXCHANGES: REDUCING EXCESS INVENTORY

The barter industry has not only dramatically widened its client base in the past few years, but it has also widened the scope of the services it offers. Some specialists in barter, *corporate trade exchanges,* now actually arrange for firms to trade their excess inventory for media and advertising time or other products and services, such as accommodations and travel for sales staff. It has proven to be a welcome alternative to going through a costly liquidation process, and it is estimated that businesses and corporations moved over $5 billion of unsold production through these types of networks in 1993.

WHO JOINS?

Although they all possess similar personality characteristics, people who make barter a part of their business tend to fall into two distinct groups: the self-employed and the company executive. Both see barter as a way of gaining the competitive edge and advancing their firm's position, but whereas someone self-employed has to convince only her/himself, the company executive usually has to sell the concept of barter to several others. The decision to join a barter network becomes more difficult as the size of the firm increases. The larger firms, which have the most to gain through a successful barter transaction, particularly those firms with complex marketing problems, are often the businesses most challenged by the idea. Once you have to talk to more than two department heads, there's a greater chance that someone will see barter as an invasion of their turf. Barter deals usually happen because someone in power has said: "This is good for us, and we'll do it. Everyone else will have to fall in line."

In spite of initial resistance, making that barter commitment has been the management style of corporations such as McDonnell Douglas, Pepsico, and IBM.

These and dozens of other household names have established their own barter departments and actively pursue deals around the world. They have placed themselves on the cutting edge, and other firms are following. Approximately 90 percent of Fortune 500 companies have some sort of proactive policy regarding barter, and many are appointing internal staff that arranges for trades of obsolete or surplus equipment and products.

It is predicted that when corporate America treats barter as seriously as Boeing or GM does, it will trigger off a revolution in the marketplace. The barter industry sees corporate barter as a sleeping giant that has just begun to stir.

INTERNATIONAL BARTER

Modern barter is not confined to the domestic marketplace. International barter, known as *countertrade*, keeps goods and services flowing between cash-starved Third World countries and the industrialized nations of the West. It not only helps Bangladesh get some badly needed imports, but it keeps American industry and labor in the business of providing them.

THE FUTURE

Domestic and international barter are not showing any signs of slowing down in their phenomenal growth curves. Since the mid-1970s, the top American barter and trading systems have consistently posted growth figures of between 100 to 400 percent per year. On the international level, barter has gone from being a government and industry irritant to a recognized way of doing business abroad. In fact, it is insisted on as a prerequisite for trade by many Third World countries.

This book is about the people who took barter out of the swap meet and into the national and international marketplace, and how they did it. They are the owner/operators who, together with their clients and the business world of America, established the nation's trade exchanges and a whole new industry.

They are people who haven't forsaken the American Dream, still want an abundant material life, and have refused to be frustrated by the economic conditions of today. They are aggressive, innovative, and a fascinating study of the archetypal American entrepreneur in action.

1

What Is the Barter Industry?

The land of barter is the land of the entrepreneur. Even the idea of trading conjures up images of tough decisions and risks-takers. In this respect, the modern barter industry hasn't changed much from the times when Vikings opened up trade routes through Russia to the Black Sea and Istanbul, trading furs and northern products for the exotic offerings of the Middle East.

In the United States there are over 450 barter systems with a total membership of 200,000 companies and individuals. This represents approximately two million Americans relying in some way on barter for their economic health. In 1993 an estimated *$8 billion* was bartered in services and products, all without cash. Barter systems have their own national organizations with their own lobbyist to represent their interests in Washington. They even have their own congressional bill, and as early as 1984, they reached a special understanding with the IRS.

BARTER NETWORK OPERATORS

Getting into the business of barter takes a certain type of individual. It's no accident that it is only the United States that barter has become a significant alternative to the domestic mainstream marketplace. The United States is the leader in barter systems because of one word: aggressive entrepreneurship. In a cash-starved society, the American entrepreneur says: "Forget the traditional way of doing things. Let's find other ways of making deals."

Barter trade exchange operators, the men and women who have built the barter industry, are a unique breed; business-smart with the bright confidence of those who know they are on to a good thing. Most have had to pay their dues in arduous apprenticeships of sixteen-hour days of selling a difficult concept to a skeptical business community. For many, their dedication has paid off handsomely. Some operators have taken their trade exchanges from zero to $1 million plus in gross income in less than six years.

Commercial barter operators can afford to pay top dollar to attract the right staff. The largest trade exchanges regularly gross $5 to $10 million annually in commissions and transaction fees and engage the best of entrepreneurial talent and management.

Ray Bastarache, president of Barter Network Inc. in Milford, Connecticut, defines successful barter systems owners as "people who don't go in for negative emotional decision making."

Fiercely independent, barter operators have managed to stick together long enough to create an entirely new marketplace and way of doing business. They've survived several scandals from the unscrupulous in their midst, skepticism from every level of the business community, and raids by a suspicious IRS.

THE GROWTH OF BARTER NETWORKS

The industry is still very young; most pinpoint 1969 as the year that systemized barter first appeared in the United States. In a multi-billion dollar industry that's less than twenty-five years old, it's to be expected that even the old hands are scarcely middle-aged and are still brimming with the fervor of a new vision of the market. The result is an industry that is still surging under the impetus of new ideas, new techniques, and new applications. The result is wide diversity.

TYPES OF BARTER SYSTEMS

As in all industries, an idea is first developed into a technique, which eventually evolves into a speciality all its own. This is certainly what happened and is continuing to happen in the barter industry. As a result of the mass of ideas and information generated daily, barter exchanges are no longer one simple concept but are now divided into six different categories, each with numerous subgroups. Each type of exchange is unique in the types of services it provides and the market need it fulfills.

Commercial Trade Exchanges

Most prolific and most easily recognizable of all barter systems are the regional and national *commercial trade exchanges*. Commercial trade exchanges account for 80 percent of all players in the barter field and are the most visible to the general public. Commercial trade exchanges serve a wide range, from a one-person book-keeping service to a modest manufacturing plant, trading products and services usually within the $50 to $15,000 range. A sampling of a firm's account with one of these trade exchanges would show purchases such as part-time secretarial services, hotel accommodations, car rentals, printing, restaurant meals, photocopiers, or landscaping services. At the higher end you might find real estate trades or large-scale construction projects, all financed through the trade credit. Even life insurance and surgery are being offered in the larger exchanges.

A commercial trade exchange keeps track of the transactions of its clients as credits and debits in trade credits, handles complaints, publishes a member directory, and provides statements for the IRS at year's end. It makes most of its profits from a small service charge on each transaction and on membership fees.

If you're in that small- to mid-size business range, looking to decrease cash flow and increase your market network and sales, a commercial trade exchange is what you would probably join.

Corporate Trade Exchanges or Trading Companies

The *corporate trade exchange* or *corporate trading company* has an entirely different format and set of goals from the commercial trade exchange. It also has a misleading title, which seems to indicate it only has large corporations as clients. In reality, the corporate trade exchange specializes in helping companies maximize their return on distressed inventory or other unwanted assets. It arranges trades for other products and services that the company does want.

Corporate trade exchanges specialize in "big-ticket" barter and customized transactions using trade credits as a bookkeeping device. There are significant differences between trade credits issued by commercial trade exchanges and corporate trade exchanges. Whereas the trade credits issued by commercial trade exchanges are backed by the goods and services of the network, the trade credits of a corporate trade exchange are essentially a promise to perform.

Corporate trade exchanges don't offer memberships or ongoing services. They act as brokers, taking their profits as a percentage of the transactions. Even though there are far fewer corporate trade exchanges than commercial ones, they do ten times the dollar volume. While commercial trade exchanges usually transact four-figure deals or less, the typical transaction in a corporate trading company often exceeds $1 million and has gone as high as $16 million. If you're a manufacturer who just doesn't know how to get rid of overruns or redundant stock, a reputable corporate trading company would be your best bet.

The Full Service Exchange

Many of the larger commercial trade exchanges, such as Chicago Barter Corporation and Barter Network Inc., are now setting up their own corporate trading divisions, producing a hybrid that also offers a trade solution to companies with distressed inventory.

Although they are in the same field of inventory clearance, these hybrids are a long way from being a serious threat to the more specialized and experienced corporate trade exchanges. They can, however, provide valuable alternatives for the smaller firm by offering greater flexibility and a greater variety of potential trades. When a midwest jeweler found himself unable to meet his bank loan, the Chicago Barter Corp. stepped into the picture. The exchange bought $100,000 worth of jewelry for one hundred thousand trade credits, which the bank accepted as payment of the debt. The bank then used the credits to buy supplies from CBC. The jewelers were saved from a crippling bankruptcy charge and the trade exchange acquired quality jewelry, which it then resold to its members.

Full service exchanges also offer variations on the more familiar one-on-one swap, with the broker taking a percentage of the action. For instance, the popular television show "Wheel of Fortune" was made possible by a commercial trade exchange that arranged for the prizes to be donated in return for advertising exposure. This type of barter creates a win-win situation—for the TV or radio station with advertising time to sell, as well as for the manufacturer who wants to get products or services in front of the public.

Countertrade

International barter has its own special name: *countertrade*. Simply put, if you want to sell your machine parts in Indonesia, the Indonesia government may require you to take part or all of your payment in copra or teak or other Indonesian products. The logic is simple. Most Third World countries don't want to see their hard currencies depleted by an excessive imbalance of imports over exports, as they insist that any import has to be *balanced* by an equal value export.

A company that specializes in putting together countertrade deals will find a hard currency market for that Indonesian teak. This preserves a balance in Indonesia's overseas earnings and ensures your payment. For the American exporter, a countertrade transaction is usually a done deal before the product even leaves the factory.

International barter attracts all sizes of players. In 1993 Pepsico announced plans to swap marketing expertise for Pizza Hut sites in the Ukraine. The turnover value for this one deal alone was in excess of $1 billion. Pepsico will help the Ukraine market its tankers and then use its commission to build a chain of Pizza Huts throughout the country. This type of barter is already an established practice in the international marketplace and the total annual value of such deals around the world, supposedly tops $1 trillion, nearly 25 percent of world trade.

But getting into the international market through countertrade is not only for the big players with high-profile products. Successful countertrade sales can be as small as a $100,000 export of wheelbarrows to Pakistan or a $200,000 export of machinery bearings to Argentina.

Although such transactions are put together differently and take longer to mature, countertrade does not mean you'll be paid in an exotic substance that you then have to market. About 99 percent of countertrade transactions finish with the exporter being paid in hard currency, just like in any other export sale.

UltraTrade

UltraTrade is not so much a new barter system but a quantum leap forward in the way barter is transacted. It is a system based on a multimillion-dollar high-tech computer program specifically developed to make simultaneous barter transfers among up to 400,000 companies. Once it goes into operation in late 1993, client companies will be able to develop incredibly intricate swaps of unused production capacity at lightning speed.

James Cargile, a vice president of the company, emphasizes that UltraTrade is not in competition with other barter systems. His target client is the large corporation with unused production capacity rather than distressed inventory. It's an area that is theoretically far outside the client groups of the commercial and corporate trade exchanges. However, UltraTrade's potential impact on American industry is bound to affect the barter world as well. Even if it is only modestly successful, this new method of simultaneous transfer of goods and services without the need for financing could generate billions in additional production capacity.

One-on-One Barter

The sixth category of barter is swapping one item for another, or *one-on-one* barter. Even this type of transaction has gone through changes as it has evolved from a simple trade involving a few hundred dollars to deals with aggregate values of hundreds of thousands or even millions of dollars. Here are a few examples of this category:

• FAVORS FOR ADVERTISING
In general, Americans believe that "Let's do business" means the same as "Let's help each other," and this can lead to barter on a grand scale. One man with this attitude saved the taxpayers hundreds of millions of

dollars and put on a party to which the whole world came. Peter V. Ueberroth appointed as president of the Los Angeles Olympic Organizing Committee, determined that the games were too high profile not to pay for themselves. So instead of asking for donations of funds only, he looked for apples-to-oranges swaps as well: prestige and media exposure were bartered in return for needed products, from food to stopwatches. As a result, the 1984 Olympics in Los Angeles were the first on record to be financed by private-sector sponsors, mainly through barter. Each sponsor had to provide the Olympics with between $4 to $13 million in cash, services, or products. In return they received the right to display the Olympic symbol and call themselves "Olympic sponsors."

Some of the thirty firms that seized the opportunity were United Airlines, Adidas, Easton Aluminum, *Sports Illustrated*, and Pageantry World Inc. They provided a range of items, from transportation for the athletes and officials, to footballs, handballs, athletic bags, arrows for competitive archery, magazine and souvenir programs, and the flags and banners that waved over the competitors and spectators. As a result of barter, the 1984 Olympics cost the taxpayers of Los Angeles only 5 percent of what Moscow spent on the 1980 spectacle.

• GAMES SHOWS

Swapping product for high exposure is not just limited to one-time shows like the Olympics. For over twenty years, Bob Robertson's company Game Show Placements Ltd., has specialized in placing products for giveaways on national television programs such as "The Price is Right" and "Jeopardy." Robertson also offers a Products-in-Film Registry for manufacturers who want to have a movie star sip their beer or wear their watch in a film.

For Bob Robertson, 63, moving into bartering products for media time was a natural segue. Twenty years ago he owned a small advertising agency, but he found it easier to move products rather than ideas. Today, he, his two sons, and five other staffers work out of their converted Spanish-style apartment building in Hollywood. His biggest headache? Getting some manufacturers to deliver their prizes as promised.

Game Show Placements works on the principle of barter leverage: it's cheaper for a company to give away its product as a prize plus a small cash fee than to buy the equivalent advertising exposure. As a bonus, expert studies say that audience retention of a product name is far greater when it is presented as a prize rather than in a thirty-second spot ad. Manufacturers obviously believe these studies. In twenty years Robertson has bartered over $12 million in products for high exposure media time for such companies as Panasonic, Chrysler, Levi Strauss, Holland American Lines, and Zenith Corporation.

• REAL ESTATE

One-on-one bartering often has the advantage of barter leverage: you're taking a product of wholesale value and directly translating it into a retail purchase. For instance, Chrysler may provide a prize at manufacturer's price but will receive advertising equivalent to its retail value.

Real estate, however, has no wholesale value and there may seem no immediate advantage to bartering it instead of trying to sell it on the open market. But swapping real estate for a property of equivalent value has become a large part of the barter industry because it eliminates the necessity of financing.

Another major reason why real estate swapping is becoming so popular is the Like-Kind tax law, which allows swaps of real estate within a similar category. If an apartment block in Miami is traded across the board for a hotel (another investment property) anywhere in the United States, some or all of the capital gains taxes may be deferred under Section 1031 of the Internal Revenue Code. Real estate swaps using Like-Kind laws (deferred exchanges) are extremely tricky, and you shouldn't attempt one without the help of a reputable and competent real estate tax expert. The most unnerving aspect of such a deal is that for a few days your real estate moves out of your hands and into the hands of an intermediary, someone known as an accommodator. If you're interested in pursuing this very attractive but potentially risky barter, your best starting point is the taxation division of your local Bar Association.

• REAL ESTATE FOR GOODS

Most of the larger commercial trade exchanges can offer advice or assistance on real estate swaps. A broker might also assist in a direct swap of other assets for real estate. Secondhand goods may not have barter leverage but can still be appealing as swap items, particularly when the traditional market for them is soft. Real estate has been swapped for just about anything the owner thinks is of roughly equivalent value: cars, boats, furs, airplanes, even a cruise for two.

• GEMSTONES FOR REAL ESTATE

Most real estate swaps for other products are easy to put together and carry little risk. They simply require close attention to detail. But scandal hit the industry with the gemstones-for-real estate swap. In 1983, Los Angeles police raided a home and found gems with an appraised value of $20 million, but an actual value of less than $200,000. The police were investigating a scam that had raked in a possible $500 million annually for three years, bilking property owners around the world.

The setup was simple. In the early 1980s, real estate was in trouble. Prices were down, but so was the market. Sellers were anxious to unload properties that seemed to have lost their value. To take advantage of the situation, a California-based gang accumulated literally tons of semiprecious gems such as rubies, opals, amethysts, sapphires—all the stones you'd see in a pirate's chest.

These gems were appraised by a "friendly" jeweler or minor appraisal laboratory that gave certificates of appraisal of up to one hundred times the gems' true value; for instance, gems that had a true value of $10 per carat were valued at $1,000 per carat. The appraisers issued gold-sealed certificates to prove the value of the gems. Then a mixture of a half-dozen or so gems were sealed in plastic with the official appraisal attached. A bag was valued at $3,000, $6,000, or up to $20,000, according to its contents. The true resale value was as low as $30, $60, or $200.

What the promoters were relying on was the public's ignorance of the gemstone market. Although it's true that some gems do have a high resale value and will appreciate through the years, investment gemstones like these are rare and difficult to spot by anyone but an expert. The promoters knew the public generally thought of gemstones in the same category as gold: uniform in value, portable, and a secure investment in times of trouble.

Searching out people who were looking to sell their real estate, the promoters would offer to take it off their hands in return for the gems. To sweeten the pot, they would barter the gems at half their appraised value. As a result, hundreds of victims parted with valuable real estate for essentially worthless gems with phony appraisals.

The crooks success in duping the public can be judged from the fact that they operated in thirteen states and six countries for three years before they were stopped. Amazingly, although several people were under suspicion, no charges were ever filed and no one was prosecuted. Anaheim police called it the largest fraud case in California's history.

The fledgling barter industry was disturbed by this potential damage to its reputation, so *Barter News*, the industry's official magazine, ran several articles by gemologists on how to spot a gemstone scam and why gems are generally not a good investment. Some insiders claim that today's deteriorating economy will give rise to a similar scam, perhaps using stamps or dubious art pieces.

BARTER AUCTIONS

Apart from the day-to-day bartering done by networks and brokers, the industry periodically sponsors barter auctions. The purpose of a barter auction is to give barterers a chance to expose their product or service and do business with each other. The medium of exchange is the trade credit. The sponsoring exchange charges an entrance fee and takes its usual transaction commission on each sale. Often the exchange will open the auction to members of other commercial trade exchanges, creating a festive market that can go on for two or three days. It's not unusual for the barterer with something to offer to get up on the podium and act as the auctioneer for his or her product or service.

A good example of an astute barterer is a Vancouver businesswoman, owner of a resort property on the coast, who used barter and her knowledge of barter auctions to finance a multimedia advertising campaign. First she designed and printed scrip for her resort, then took it to a barter auction that was being promoted regularly by a commercial trade exchange in Oregon. Her accommodation scrip was snapped up by bidders eager for the chance to use their trade credits for an unusual holiday destination.

With several thousand dollars in trade credits, she then researched media and print outlets that belonged to barter networks. One outlet was *Benefits,* a California publication mailed to companies with over fifty employees that specializes in listing possible employee benefits. From *Benefits* alone she received hundreds of inquiries.

She tempers her enthusiasm for barter with some sensible words: "The main advice I could give anyone joining barter is to stay on your toes. Barter seems to bring out the best and the worst in people, and you have to stay sharp. Don't accumulate too many trade credits if you don't know where to spend them, and when you see a deal, don't hesitate. Barter isn't like the cash marketplace, where there's almost an unlimited supply of deals for people with money."

She tells people to reject the idea that barter is difficult to understand: "Barter is like going to a foreign country. At first the money seems quaint and the local customs are different. But if you stay there for a while, you realize everyone's doing the same thing as back home, except in a slightly different manner."

THE BUSINESS NETWORK

There are other advantages to trade exchange membership that are not so obvious. One, frequently quoted, is that barter systems bring together individuals who are commercially compatible. For instance, four years ago when Herb Maddock enrolled his fledgling landscaping business in The Barter Group in Phoenix, he was hoping for the usual deals on automotive repairs and so on.

"People who join barter clubs tend to have a similar outlook on business and on life. We support each other but sometimes I suspect it's not just for the economics. We tend to like each other as well."

They also educate each other. Herb tells the story of one new member who had amassed quite a few trade credits in a short time but was complaining he didn't know what to do with them.

"At the same time, he was saying how much he'd like to take the family to California for a vacation. I pointed out that my family had just got back from a four-day vacation in California where we'd stayed at $75-a-night hotels and eaten in the best restaurants—all on trade credits. When he heard that, he suddenly got the message that trade credits are for *spending,* but you have to be aggressive in finding the market."

Maddock spends his trade credits in typical ways: new carpeting for his house, renovations to turn the double garage into a third bedroom/den, vacations to such destinations as Mexico and across the United States, auto repairs, hearing aids for a relative, and eating out.

"If we could find a baby-sitter who takes trade credits we'd eat out every week," he says whimsically.

Maddock estimates his annual trading volume as about $12,000 with The Barter Group and about $5,000 with Barter Exchange International (BXI), which he joined last year. Why two memberships?

"First, I like to have as many purchase options as I can. More members mean more services and product, more things to spend my trade credits on. Second, of course, more members mean more exposure for my business. In a barter system, I may be one landscaper among two or three competitors. And I know that people will drive that extra mile to do business with trade credits rather than cash. I certainly do."

THE COMPETITIVE EDGE

Trade exchange clients often stress that bartering is not just about the fun things in life, it can also provide the competitive edge that means the difference between a business's survival or demise. Angus McDonald of Houston markets commercial air purification systems. He claims that his ability to survive the tough first year of business was solely because he could use his barter credits for hotel rooms, restaurants, and other travel expenses.

"My barter club ticket was a lifeline in more ways than one," he says. "Not only could I offset a lot of my startup expenses, which involved an awful lot of traveling, but I also had an immediate solid base of business contacts who bought my product through barter. What I was expecting from my barter group was entirely different than what I got. I had hoped to maybe get a discount here and there or maybe get a haircut occasionally. Instead, I found I was plugged into a network that spread over three states—and they were interested in what I was offering. Barterers tend to look within their own system first, and every bit of advertising I wrote got some response. For the first six months of business at least three quarters of my income was in trade credits, and I spent them all."

For the price of his membership, McDonald had found a ready market for his product and a tight club of people bonded by one common attitude: a determination that in spite of the economic news, business is as usual.

IMAGE PROBLEMS

United States business and industry have the mechanisms in place to power a significant revival in the economy. Estimates for untapped trading through domestic trade exchanges and corporate trading alone range from $400 billion to $700 billion. At the extreme end, proponents of UltraTrade claim that a complete utilization of untapped domestic trading capabilities would generate over $1 trillion in increased business.

On the international scene, countertrade is the marketing tool that can provide the United States with a resurgence in exports and the means to recapture the lead position in trade growth. With a resurgence in export business comes an increase in profits and an increase in jobs. Bartering, international and domestic, is legal, profitable, and carries no more risks than any other marketplace venture. So why isn't everybody joining in?

Well, not all negative attitudes toward barter are due to lack of information or clear thinking, or due to business timidity. Behind the smoke and mirrors image of the industry is enough real fire to make anyone cautious of getting burned. Growth has been impressively, but the barter industry is still struggling with a negative public image, largely an inheritance from the past. In the early

1970s, when barter exchanges were just emerging in the marketplace, bad deals, scams, and outright fraud gave the industry a shady reputation from which it still hasn't recovered.

Even today, not all the players have been redeemed, and the industry's present reputation still suffers from the odd scandal. Two national organizations, the National Association of Trade Exchanges (NATE) and the International Reciprocal Trade Association (IRTA), are trying to combat the situation with a code of ethics and operating standards, public education, and self-policing. These are all sorely needed. Today's barter industry is no longer a simple, quaint addendum to the marketplace. It has grown into a complex of interlocking barter systems, each fulfilling distinct and unique roles. As the needs of American business grows, so will barter's size, complexity, and need for complete professionalism.

ECONOMIC BILINGUALISM

How significant is the barter industry to the future of North America's marketplace? John Madsen, owner of Vancouver-based Bartercard and founder of the Canadian International Trade Exchange Organization, sums up the situation of barter in the world's economy:

"Barter is growing so fast and in so many different directions that individuals and corporations need to learn to operate in both the money market and the barter one. I call it learning 'economic bilingualism'—being fluent in both types of trade. Whatever happens in the future, the smart businessman will be able to talk in both languages."

2
Why Barter?

Although systemized barter expands during up-swings in the economy, much of barter's success is linked to the times when the nation's money supply becomes so inadequate that any alternative is welcomed. By using trade credits to "monetize" the assets of their members, barter systems create another medium of exchange and an alternative source of money for the nation.

THE NATION'S DWINDLING MONEY SUPPLY

Do we really need such an alternative? Has our nation's money supply become inadequate for our needs? The answer seems to be yes. Although reluctantly, many economists are now facing up to the connection between money supply and economic depression; in fact, they've even given it a name: debt-liquidation deflation. This describes a situation that appears when so much money is being used to repay public and private debt that little is left for the normal running of industry and the marketplace.

The cycles of debt-liquidation deflation have been brilliantly described by Harry Schultz, an international investment analyst and publisher of the newsletter *HSL.* The *Guiness Book of World Records* lists him as the world's highest-paid investment consultant, and at $2,400 an hour, they could be right. One reason Schultz is so highly paid is his ability for the past twenty years to forecast correctly every significant shift in the world economy.

Schultz credits his record of solid economic forecasts to the writings of Dr. Thomas McGrath who perceived that economic depressions followed periods of excessive credit expansion. He claims that every bout of borrowing is followed by a period of tight money—you have to stop spending until you've paid off the loan.

The connection between the rate of money creation and economic depressions has been a background theme for fringe economics ever since the Underconsumptionists of the late nineteenth century, who claimed there is never enough money in any society to adequately furnish its needs. They said that money creation always lagged behind production, and ultimately production would be forced to stop because of unsold inventory.

However, the connection between money supply and economic depression didn't become a respectable theory until the 1960s when Nobel laureate Milton Friedman proposed his "monetarist" version of economics. In a variation of McGrath's theory, Friedman said that economic depressions and recessions invariably followed a constriction of money growth. The constriction could stem from several reasons: high interest rates, too much public and private debt. Although still not regarded as mainstream economics, Friedman may yet be vindicated if present theories continue to be inadequate.

HOW DOES MONEY DWINDLE?

We don't often think of money as growing in ways other than through hard work, but actually the money supply of the United States changes daily through decisions made between the Federal Reserve Board and the government. Balancing new money coming into the economy with money going out is like trying to keep a bathtub filled with water with both the tap running and the plug open. The chief method of encouraging money growth is through low interest rates that stimulate more borrowing, leading to more money being created to meet the demand. The tap is running. On the other hand, high interest rates suck money out of the system through debt repayment. High rates also restrict the borrowing of money by making it more expensive. With less money in the marketplace there is less available buying power. Friedman claimed that a prolonged period of tight money eventually has an impact on industry and the wage sector, putting the economy in a self-perpetuating downward spiral.

It's a scenario that has had trouble gaining majority support within the establishment. Many economists still prefer to think of "hidden hands" within the economy that just make things happen. They argue over the chicken and egg theory—whether lack of money gives rise to economic depressions, or vice versa—but the facts are that the rate of money creation has become insufficient to keep up with the nation's demand. The entire marketplace economy has reversed itself, and instead of credit expansion boom times, we have a credit contraction depression. It happens in the best of households when payments to Visa and the bank and the mortgage company become so great that there's nothing left for a trip to Hawaii or even a night out at McDonald's.

The statistics to support Friedman's arguments are impressive. Every collapse of the economy over the past hundred years has been preceded by a sharp drop in money creation (running the tap) or a high increase in interest rates (opening the plug). Debt is sucking money out of the economy faster than business and the banking system can pump it back in. How long this state of affairs will continue is impossible to predict, but the last time it happened was during the Great Depression of the 1930s. It went on for ten years until massive credit expansion and spending to finance World War II broke the cycle.

HOW A DWINDLING MONEY SUPPLY CREATES A BARTER OPPORTUNITY

At ground level we see the immediate results of money deflation as shrinking markets and plant closures. Because the consumer is busy paying off debts instead of buying, industry soon finds itself with unsold inventory—the first step toward cutbacks and closure. As the work force loses confidence in its future it cuts back on expenditures, making the soft market even softer. The industry-marketplace cycle goes into a downward spin and the economy slows almost to a halt. Hard times have started. While governments are busy talking about what causes economic depressions and how to fix them, one practical reality is that we are running out of money.

All of this directly affects the man and woman in the street, and it helps explain why barter systems are leaping forward in popularity. Barter has many appealing aspects, but today its chief attraction is as a substitute for ready cash. Barter systems create their own "cash" with trade credits. They may not be real dollars, but they serve the same purpose. If someone wants to buy or sell, a barter system instantly creates the credits needed to make it happen.

NEW WAYS OF ECONOMIC SURVIVAL THROUGH BARTER

Today's economy is so challenging, even for the most innovative, that the best many can do is hang on grimly, waiting until money and the traditional marketplace reappears. But some Americans have seized the challenge that a tight money economy presents and have found new ways of surviving, even prospering, by developing new methods of doing business. Often this means developing new behavioral patterns, new relationships, new ways of thinking.

When American entrepreneurs found the money in their pocket was inadequate, bartering their goods and services became the next logical step. By networking and bartering for their needs and luxuries they still maintain their life-styles in spite of what's happening out there. They still provide goods and services for others and they still get what they want in return. The only difference for these survivors is that they now operate in two economic worlds: the world of the dollar and the world of the trade credit.

REAL MONEY COSTS OF BARTER

Are the two worlds really that separate, or is there a cash money cost for bartering? Well, yes, it does cost money to barter. For one thing there is the cost of providing your product. Whether it is simple overhead for giving a haircut or a considerable outlay for the manufacture of a thousand patio tables, there is always the real money cost of what you are offering within the network.

Then there are the fees and sign-up costs for the network itself. The fees are charged on each transaction that goes through your account. Transaction fees can range from 5 percent to 13 percent according to the network and your particular contract. These fees are usually but not always in cash, not trade credits. Other payments to the network might include the interest on any loans you take out. Even if your loan is in trade credits, you will usually have to repay the interest itself in cash. Monthly service charges are also being introduced by some exchanges and these are usually paid in cash.

Another cash outlay is taxes. The IRS has had an agreement for the past ten years with barter networks. All transactions must be reported as cash transactions and are taxed at year's end along with the rest of your business revenue.

All in all, barter is not the simple cashless transaction that many people think it is. However, it is a transaction that needs a lot *less* cash, and this is what makes the difference. For the business that can't find a market for its product, barter offers the chance to change a liability into a needed asset for a minimal cash outlay. It's an appeal that is proving popular to more and more of business America.

DISCRETIONARY SPENDING AND BARTER

For American business, the trade credit alternative to the traditional money system works particularly well in the area of *discretionary spending.* Do you remember the good old days of "discretionary spending"—the cute term the admen thought up to describe disposable income, mad money, discretionary dollars, play money, the money left in our pockets after all the bills are paid?

Whether you're a consumer or business mogul, discretionary money is fun money. We know we have it when we tap our teeth with a pencil and dream of the nice things we are going to buy ourselves, the kids, or the business. When you say to yourself: "A trip to Houston could expand our dealers in that area," you're thinking in discretionary spending terms. All you need is an airplane ticket, three nights at a hotel, and some meals. Barter exchanges excel at providing these types of services and products. They allow you to directly exchange your own product or service for that airline ticket, hotel room, and meals at a restaurant. You don't have to wait for the marketplace and its buy, save, spend routine. With barter, you access your discretionary purchasing power immediately.

Discretionary spending is the same at all levels of business: it's spending you can manipulate according to income. For instance, any ad firm will tell you that advertising is absolutely imperative, but in reality it's discretionary spending. Corporate trade exchanges fill their market niche by swapping your excess inventory for equal value advertising; in other words, they convert your inventory into discretionary spending power that you spend on advertising.

IMPERATIVE SPENDING AND BARTER

At one time, all trade exchanges were concerned with discretionary spending, but these days their offerings are far more diverse and sophisticated. Barter systems are stepping in and arranging deals that are intimately concerned with daily survival, the imperative side of the ledger. If you're saying to yourself, "I'd better deal with this bill from Charlie's Trucking before they cut us off," it's highly likely that a barter network in your area has an alternative trucking company that you can pay with trade credits rather than cash. One network of trade exchanges has even negotiated for members to pay a portion of their AT&T bills with trade credits.

THE TRADE CREDIT, SECRET OF MODERN BARTER

The key to understanding the complex world of modern barter is the trade credit, a bookkeeping device that allows firms to keep an accurate accounting of barter transactions. The trade credit used by commercial trade exchanges allows a hairdressing salon to swap its latest styling for auto parts or a ski holiday in Colorado. The trade credit used by corporate trade exchanges is different. It is what the manufacturer receives for his distressed inventory instead of cash. The corporate trade exchange issues the trade credits, then oversees their spending on prearranged product or service.

How a Trade Credit Works

In simplest terms, a barter system acts as the "honest broker" between clients by keeping credit and debit accounts of all the transactions that take place. These accounts are kept in *trade dollars*, also known as *trade credits*. Each trade credit theoretically holds the same value as a cash dollar; each transaction is valued as if it were a normal wholesale or retail transaction.

Creation of Trade Credits

Trade credits start their lives as loans or lines of credit. Commercial trade exchanges loan trade credits to their members, but as with any line of authorized credit, such as at a department store, the trade exchange doesn't really *loan* you trade credits at all. It simply opens your account and allows purchases up to the negotiated loan limit. If you ask for a loan of $T1,000, the exchange merely has to note in the credit side of your ledger that you have been authorized to incur a debt of that amount. By extending this line of credit to you, the trade exchange creates new trade credits for your use, which you must pay back at some time. It then charges you for keeping track of how you spend them. In brief, the barter industry runs on a money supply that it creates itself.

A common question asked by those who are interested in the mechanisms of a trade exchange is, who does the trade credit ultimately belong to? Since the exchange has created it, it might seem that the trade credit belongs to the exchange, but this is not true. The International Reciprocal Trade Association (IRTA) fact sheet on trade credits makes it quite clear that the credits are a function of the clients' assets, not the exchange. The practical result of this is that if an exchange collapses, leaving you with $T500 in your account, there is no way to force the operator to redeem trade credits for cash.

Nominal Value of Trade Credits

When you join a trade exchange, you must agree to accept other members' trade credits in place of cash. When you are using your trade credits to buy or sell within the exchange, you'll fix your pricing exactly as you would in the outside world. If your fee in the outside world is $100, then you're expected to charge $T100 within the system. If your product normally retails for $500, you're expected to charge $T500 to your fellow barterers. Once you've agreed on these two simple rules, you are ready to make a transaction.

EXAMPLE OF A TRANSACTION

Let us suppose you are a manufacturer of gas appliances and have an excess inventory of thirty water heaters. They may be out of date or simple victims of poor marketing or a sluggish economy. These heaters retail for $2,000 each. They cost you $1,000 to manufacture and normally wholesale at $1,500. To you they represent a total investment of $30,000 and a possible profit of $15,000.

Now let us also suppose you have a warehouse that needs rewiring and you'd like to make some additions to the mezzanine floor. You've got the bids, and it looks like the entire job, carpentry and electrical, will cost about $30,000.

In a normal business climate you would simply factor the costs of the renovations, probably take out a bank loan to cover the work, hire an electrician and a carpenter, and get the job done. You would finance the alterations out of the sale of your heaters. At a profit of

$500, selling sixty heaters would completely pay off the cost of the warehouse alterations.

But the heaters aren't finding their market, and you don't want to risk taking out yet another loan just to get the warehouse fixed. So let's consider another option: swapping the heaters you have for the electrical and carpentry work you need. If you could find an electrician and a carpenter to go along with the idea, at the wholesale price of your heaters, $1,500 each, you'd have to swap only twenty heaters to "pay" for all the work you want done on the warehouse.

You could accomplish several things. First, you would reduce your distressed inventory by moving twenty heaters out of your warehouse and off your books. Second, you'd have a renovated warehouse. Third, your real cost of the renovations would not be $30,000 as quoted, but $20,000—your manufacturing cost of the heaters.

BARTER LEVERAGE: BUY WHOLESALE, SELL RETAIL

In this case, consider your manufacturing costs as your wholesale price; that is, by bartering your heaters for labor and materials you will be paying only $20,000 cash for renovations that have a retail value of $30,000. By using trade credits instead of cash, you will actually save yourself a cash outlay of $10,000. In the industry's shorthand, this saving is known as *barter leverage*. It happens whenever a barter deal saves real cash outlay and is the reason why barterers say they "buy wholesale and sell retail." Barter leverage has many different applications, which we'll go over in detail later in this chapter.

Bartering your heaters for warehouse repairs is a good idea. The challenge, of course, is to find an electrician and a carpenter who want to swap twenty heaters for the work. Trade exchanges are designed precisely around this sort of problem and have set up multiparty exchanges.

Let's assume that you already belong to the Crosspoint Commercial Trade Exchange. As a member, you have their directory listing all the products and services available from members, including several carpenters and electricians, who you call and ask for quotes. You find two who will do the entire renovation for $T30,000—the equivalent of the cash quote you got earlier.

Now you are faced with a choice. You can either take out a bank loan of $30,000 or take out a loan with Crosspoint for $T30,000. It is a fairly straightforward decision to make. A bank loan will have to be repaid in cash; a loan from the exchange will have to be repaid in trade credits. Will it be easier to find the cash for repayment or trade credits? In other words, will you be able to sell your heaters more easily on the open market for cash or sell them to exchange members for trade credits?

Opting for a loan from the exchange has one clear benefit, and that is you don't have to continue trying to sell your heaters on the open market. By offering you a loan, the exchange is counting on you to sell your heaters within the system and get trade credits to pay them back. From a no-hope situation you are now faced with the possibility that the heaters can actually be traded for something of equal value, and that you'll be able to recover some of your investment.

BARTER APPEAL

At this point, a natural question might be: "Why would it be easier to sell the heaters within the barter system rather than on the open market?" After all, if the heaters were in your warehouse because they were outmoded, they're hardly likely to be more appealing because they're being offered in barter.

But barter does make them more appealing, mainly because of barter leverage. For many clients in the trade exchange, your asking price of $T1,500 represents a *real cash* outlay to them of much less. They, too, have accumulated their trade credits by selling at retail price an item for which they have only paid wholesale or production costs. For instance, a restaurateur typically fixes prices at about double actual cash costs. To accumulate $T1,500 for one of your heaters would require a cash outlay of half that amount; that is, $750.

To buy a heater similar to yours on the open market would cost the restaurateur at least $1,500 *cash.* By buying it through the exchange, the real cash outlay for the restaurateur is only $750. At that price, the demand is bound to be hot, and why shouldn't it be? The members are getting brand-new heaters at genuine manufacturer's prices and at a real cash cost of far less than the regular retail price. It's likely you'll sell not twenty, but all thirty of your unwanted inventory.

COLLATERAL AND LOANS

There remains the possibility that your heaters won't market any better within the exchange than in the open market. If that happens, and you can't repay the loan, the exchange will possibly take possession and market them through other channels. Putting up some form of collateral for a trade credit loan is becoming an industry standard, as are other conditions, such as a time limitation for repayment and interest charges (usually paid in cash rather than trade credits). If it all sounds very similar to taking out a bank loan, it is.

SNAGS

So, what are the snags so far? One drawback is the lack of wide choice. In the cash marketplace, wide choice is taken for granted, but in barter you have to learn to work with what's available. You may find that the only electrician available has obnoxious personal habits, or charges more than you expected to pay, or just isn't available at the times you want.

Restricted availability can also be a problem. It is common among some barter clients, particularly those who specialize in seasonal goods or services such as tax consultants, to limit their availability to their off-hours or off-season. It can also happen with tradespeople, who will usually put a cash opportunity ahead of one for barter. You could possibly line everything up only to have your electrician beg off for a couple of weeks while he tends to a cash job. It doesn't happen often, but it certainly happens.

Supposing, however, you find a carpenter and an electrician who are ready and eager for your contract. With your trades lined up and your loan in your account you can now start the renovation. There's very little difference between this and any other building contract. You'll pay your trades in exactly the same manner as you would pay any contractor—by check. The only difference is that your checks are drawn on your account at the trade exchange, not your local bank, and they're written in trade credits, not dollars.

The routine for their clearance is the same as at a bank. The contractors will deposit your checks for credit into their accounts and the trade exchange will debit your account. It's quite possible that the electrician and carpenter will use some of your trade credits to buy some of their supplies for your job—lumber, saw blades, sheet rock, electrical conduits, and so on. Once again, they'll pay by check to their suppliers, who'll deposit the checks with the trade exchange.

What are your chances of being ripped off in this transaction, particularly with regard to the quality of work? Experience seems to show that the chances are slight; in fact, in an informal survey, no one reported any dissatisfaction with work done for barter rather than cash.

At some time you're going to have to repay the loan by selling off the heaters. One way to market them would be to advertise in the exchange's monthly bulletin, which goes to every client within the system. Another way would be to cold call prospective buyers. The exchange will also help by advertising your heaters through their brokers, who keep in regular contact with clients. Marketing a service or product in a commercial trade exchange is all familiar territory, with one important difference: when you advertise you'll be talking about trade credits instead of dollars. In this case, your heaters are $T1,500 apiece.

The actual sale of your heaters to an exchange member is just like any other big ticket sale. You'll be paid in credit; either by check or a special "credit card" issued by the exchange. If you want to check up on the person who's buying, you can phone for a credit check with the barter system's head office (some exchanges insist that any sale over $T50 be authorized). To make it easy for everyone, many exchanges have installed twenty-four-hour credit verification lines, which you access through a code number.

As in any open market sale, you send the records of the sales to the network's head offices for processing, just as you submit your checks or credit card slips to your bank. At the head office, your sales are credited to your account, paying off your loan of $T30,000. You will have to sell twenty heaters to do it.

Also, you are going to have to pay the exchange interest payments on your loan and transaction payments on the sale of your heaters. Has it all been worth it?

FINANCIAL SUMMARY

Suppose the Crosspoint Trade Exchange charges 10 percent interest on the $T30,000 loan for the mezzanine renovation. Your cash outlay for interest will be $3,000. On top of that, Crosspoint also asks for a 5 percent transaction fee on each heater you sell, and this will cost you an additional $1,500 in cash. Is it worth it to market twenty hard-to-sell heaters and get a $30,000 mezzanine renovation for a total cash outlay of $4,500? Of course it is.

What are the risks you take? The greatest one is that you may not be able to sell the heaters to the exchange members. It is a reduced risk in comparison to the open market, but it is still a valid one. If you fail, you may have to forfeit whatever collateral you negotiated with the exchange. Another risk might be in the quality of workmanship or materials. Both risks, however, are not unusual in the normal course of business in the open market and are mitigated by the special business environment common to successful trade exchanges—the buoyant market.

BARTER'S OWN MARKETPLACE

The comparative ease with which barterers can find markets for their products and services within the system proves the axiom that *when there is a means of exchange freely available, the market responds.*

Abundant Credit

Barter keeps trade moving because it eliminates a vital step in normal trade: getting the money together. Marketplaces require three basics: buyers, sellers, and a money unit to keep track of who owes what to whom. Barter systems make it all possible by creating their own brand of money, the trade credit, and their own marketplace. By using a fictitious money unit to keep score, barterers can freely swap services and products among themselves, and even between other trade exchanges, basically creating their own marketplace, which isolates them from the sluggishness of the mainstream economy. In today's tight-money market being able to eliminate the need to finance a trade by substituting trade credits means a boom economy, just as an expanding money supply at the beginning of World War II carried the United States out of the Depression.

New members in a commercial trade exchange are usually advanced an interest-free line of credit to get them started, and as a result of this and the easy availability of loans, the barter market never suffers from a lack of "money." People either have the means to buy or can quickly get it.

The buoyant market typical of the barter world is a stunning rebuttal of market theorists who say that people with money want to buy things, and those without money have resigned themselves to going without. Your own personal experience soon shows how wrong this belief can be. None of us stop wanting things just because we don't have money in our pockets, and the trade credit enables us to get back in the marketplace. By creating their own currency, barter systems create their own buoyant market, which is quite separate from the national economy.

Preference and Restricted Competition

Apart from abundant credit, the barter marketplace has two other appealing aspects: a preference for barter and restricted competition.

Would you prefer to pay for something with cash or trade your own service or product for it? Invariably the answer is trade. Even if you had the money to buy what you want, in most cases you'd prefer to trade something you have or something you can do. The simple fact that people prefer trade over cash purchases makes for a looser, more active market.

The customer in the open marketplace can select from a vast range of product and services, but in a commercial trade exchange these choices are quite limited. There may be only four dentists, three Japanese restaurants, and six printers, three of whom are over ten miles away.

Limited choices like these are seen as a downside for shoppers but a boon if you are selling. For instance, if you are the only chiropractor in an exchange of one thousand members, you'll not only have better exposure than in the outside world but, because you accept trade credits, you'll be the chiropractor of preference. In brief, commercial trade exchanges offer decreased competition.

SELLING IN A TRADE EXCHANGE

Demand for good products and services in a trade exchange is always high, which makes a difference in how clients market themselves. In the open market, a great amount of energy is used in marketing a service or product: every businessperson must fill the dual roles of production management and sales. For example, a hairdresser not only has to cut hair but also has to think of ways to entice new customers and hang on to established ones. A manufacturer of lawn furniture not only has to oversee the production line but has to find ways of making the product visible in the marketplace.

Selling in a barter marketplace takes far less time and energy because restricted competition and a small range of choice make it a sellers' market. The exchange itself also promotes the needs and products of its members because it wants to keep a high trading volume.

Limited Use of the Trade Credit

Using trade credits instead of cash changes the marketplace motivations of those involved in barter. Trade credits generally enable people to conserve cash rather than make direct profits.

You can't use trade credits to pay taxes or play on the international finance scene. Bartering won't give you the money to pay off your car loan, although it will help you to save the money to do that. Barter is basically concerned with one thing only: getting the product or service you want, now. If you are only looking for cash, then bartering may not be for you. Thinking of trade credits purely as a medium of exchange is quite a perceptual shift, but a very necessary one. In the regular market-place the emphasis is on the money side of the ledger; in barter, the emphasis is on the deal.

Barter Leverage

Barter leverage, mentioned earlier in this chapter, is the advantage obtained through using barter and trade credits instead of cash. The advantage may be an easier market, or it may be buying retail at wholesale costs. Mainly, barter leverage is defined as the *difference* between the *true cost* of the trade credit (or dollar) as compared to cash.

THE TRUE COST OF A TRADE DOLLAR

How much is a trade dollar really worth? The answer is, whatever you paid for it. If it cost you 50 cents to get one trade dollar, then that trade dollar has a value to you of 50 cents, even though it is worth a full $1 within the barter network. In this respect, a trade dollar is no different than a loss leader coupon that costs you $2.50 to buy but which the supermarket will redeem for a $5 can of coffee. Calculating the cost of a trade credit is a simple matter of dividing real cash costs by the selling price. If an article costs you $75 cash to produce and you sell it for $T100, then the real cash cost to you of each trade dollar is only 75 cents. The real bargains in barter come from understanding barter leverage: the actual cash cost of a trade dollar.

Cash Costs of One Heater
  (your real costs) $1,000
Trade Credit Price of One Heater
  (your selling price) $T1,500

Each Trade Credit Costs You

$$\frac{1,000}{1,500} = 66 \text{ cents}$$

    An example of barter leverage and the true cost of a trade dollar is what could happen if you sold the other ten heaters from your excess inventory. The sale will give you a positive balance in your account of $T15,000, which you can now spend within the network. As a businessperson you may want to spend your trade credits on office equipment, printing, or advertising for your new line of heaters. Or you may decide on a two-week bonus trip for your top staff to Mexico. Most major trade exchanges would have no difficulty providing any of these services or products.

    As it is, you simply decide to go shopping and see what catches your eye. You open the monthly bulletin and find that someone is advertising a Camaro for sale for exactly $T15,000. It's a car you've always wanted but you know that a similar model can be bought for $12,000 cash on the outside market. Would you buy it?

    Analysis of the situation will make you realize that even at its inflated trade credit price, the Camaro is still a good deal. Remember, you got your $T15,000 for an actual *cash* outlay of only $10,000, the manufacturing costs of your heaters. In real money terms, each trade dollar has cost you only *66 cents cash.* You can afford to pay $T15,000 for the Camaro because in real money this represents an outlay of only $10,000. It's barter leverage again—bartering has converted thirty heaters of unknown market value into $42,000 of assets for you.

Manufacturing costs of 30 heaters @ 1,000 ea.	$30,000
Interest charges on 30,000 trade credits	3,000
5% transaction charges on sale of 30 heaters	2,250
Total cash outlay	$35,250

Cash Value of Assets

Mezzanine renovations	$30,000
One Camaro, actual value	12,000
Total value of new assets	$42,000

To sum up, you've just completed a multiparty swap. You have managed to swap your heaters for renovations of your warehouse without any cash at all except for interest payments on your loan and transaction fees. And your real cost for the renovations was only $24,500 instead of the original quote of $30,000. In addition, you've swapped the rest of your distressed inventory, which had cost you $10,000, for a car worth $12,000. By bartering plus an extra $5,250 in cash you have changed a $30,000 investment *loss* in the heaters into $42,000 worth of *desirable assets.* It is particularly worthwhile at this stage to remember that the heaters could not find their market and there was a strong possibility they would never have sold.

THE CASH COST OF A TRADE CREDIT

Doug Dagenais of Chicago Barter Corporation, an enthusiastic proponent of leverage who often lectures businesspeople on the importance of defining the real cash cost of a trade credit, has this to say:

"Businesspeople often get hung up on how their present supplier gives them best value for money. They look in the exchange directory, see that the prices they'll have to pay for their supplies are perhaps the same or occasionally even more than regular retail. It doesn't matter that the prices are in trade dollars—what they see is that prices are not the bargains they are used to looking for. For instance, a firm may have spent a year finding the cheapest supply of office stationery in town. There's been a lot of effort invested, and there's a lot of resistance to switching to a barter client who may be charging more than their present supplier. For example, a supplier may be providing you with computer paper at $4 a box. Why switch to a supplier who charges $T5 a box, even if they do take trade dollars? On the surface, it doesn't make sense. No one wants to pay regular retail prices when they already have a bargain supplier. Well, the answer's in knowing the real cash value of your trade credit."

Dagenais points out that the real cash cost of a one-dollar trade credit may be as low as 50 cents, in which case a box of computer paper at $T5.00 has a real cash cost of only $2.50.

Dagenais preaches tirelessly about barter leverage and insists that any company joining a trade exchange should calculate the actual cost of each trade dollar it earns.

"If the purchasing department knows that one hundred trade credits represent an actual cash outlay of only sixty or seventy dollars, then they're really motivated to look for suppliers within the system. If they understand that each trade dollar represents recovered money that would otherwise have been a loss, then they will really wake up to the advantages of barter."

RECOVERING THE UNRECOVERABLE

The motivation to get and spend trade dollars is even greater when a purchasing department realizes that each trade dollar is usually converted from a cash outlay that's already been made and *may never be recoverable under other circumstances*. In fact, much of the purchasing power recouped through barter is actually *free*. For example, if a product has cost $75 to produce but has become *unsalable in the regular market*, then using it successfully for barter represents a 100 percent return on the dollar. It is free purchasing power.

In the heaters example, in which you bartered a $30,000 cash investment of unwanted inventory into $42,000 worth of assets, you got more than your money back on an investment that possibly you would not have been able to liquidate except for pennies on the dollar. Instead of posting a loss on the heaters, your firm could now point to increased assets. It's a winning formula, which can be duplicated by just about any business that has unsold time or product on its hands. A hotel has empty rooms; a restaurant prepares for more meals than it will sell; a trailer manufacturer has unsold trailers; an airline has vacant seats; a clothing store has unsold inventory; an accountant has spare time.

All of these businesses pay out cash without any real hope of return. A hotel room that is not rented still needs a cash investment to cover its part of the general carrying costs: cleaning, heating, staff, and so on. Under normal marketplace conditions there is no mechanism for recovering that lost cash investment. Using barter, however, the hotel management can not only recover that lost investment but actually increase its assets and bottom line profitability.

For instance, a restaurant has certain fixed costs that apply to a table whether or not customers are actually using it. There are the costs of the kitchen, the staff, and the lease. If barter can be used to bring in customers to fill those chairs, the restaurant will be recouping some of its investment. And, as often happens in these cases, there is a good chance that new customers from barter will bring in cash paying friends.

One owner of a suntanning salon packaged her spare hours as an "Escape to the Sun" mini-vacation. It was used as a promotion by a local radio station that bartered advertising time for it. The advertising was so successful that the owner had to cut back on the bartering; she had no more spare hours to trade.

ASSETS TO CASH RECOVERY RATIO

Barter leverage is sometimes defined in terms of ratio of assets to cash: six dollars in assets for a four-dollar investment, for instance. The assets: cash recovery on the heaters was $42,000 in assets from an investment of $35,250 cash. That's a ratio of $7 worth of assets recovered for every $5.4 invested. The suntanning salon owner estimated her return as about 2:1; she recovered $2 in assets for every $1 that was trapped as fixed costs. If the fixed costs of a hotel room is $10 and this can be converted to $T50, then the hotel is receiving $50 of value for every $10 invested: a 5:1 return on your money.

Barter leverage only applies, of course, when you have spare time or product that you're paying for whether you sell it or not. If the hairdresser had as many cash clients as he or she could handle, then there'd be little point in bartering. The Flamingo Hotel and Casino in Las Vegas has a 95 percent occupancy rate, which moves it outside the category of benefitting from barter—or does it?

Barter leverage can be applied in all sorts of situations. A hotel has certain fixed costs on its rooms, which it must meet even if they're not occupied. Let's suppose that those fixed costs are $10 per room. An artist arrives with some paintings but no cash, so the hotel owner says, "I will *give* you an $80 room in my hotel for two weeks and allow you to exhibit your paintings in my lobby. In return I'd like this one painting, which has a price tag of $1,000."

The artist does some quick calculations and realizes he is getting a great chance for exposure and two weeks accommodation that would normally cost him $1,120 in return for a painting that cost him $100 in paint and a week of his time.

The hotel owner is also making some calculations. The fixed costs for the room he is giving the artist are costing him fourteen nights at $10 a night. For $140 he is getting a painting with an asking price of $1,000. In addition, he can look forward to extra restaurant and bar trade not only from the artist but from the people who will come to view his paintings. Even at 95 percent occupancy the owner knows he's going to lose money on those few empty rooms. Through barter, however, he will not only more than cover the costs of his room but he will become the owner of an art piece that could possibly increase in value over coming years.

Obviously the artist also has to acknowledge that it's unlikely he will sell all his work for cash. He has spare art, which may take months or years to sell if he doesn't take this chance, right now, to convert it into something valuable to himself.

If it all sounds rather farfetched, consider the case of

Arnold Ashkenazy, Los Angeles hotelier and entrepreneur. Back in 1986, he and his brother Severyn had already managed to accumulate over twenty thousand pieces of art valued at over $25 million, mainly through bartering rooms and exposure at one of their posh hotels. The brothers offered the deal to both struggling and established artists: rooms, room service, and limousines, and the chance to exhibit in the foyers and restaurants of their hotels—all in return for selected pieces of artwork. It was a case of classical barter leverage working at its best. For a possible total cash outlay of less than $1 million in accommodation and services (that would have normally been written off as operating expenses) the Ashkenazy brothers acquired $25 million in artwork. The artists got unparalleled exposure at a fraction of what it would have cost them in a cash market, simply by bartering.

NEW MARKET PENETRATION

There are many ways of using barter leverage and every major trade exchange has examples to show what can be done. One technique that works on an international as well as a local level is to use the promise of barter in order to penetrate a new market. For instance, suppose you are a painting contractor who wants to get the maintenance contract on a local chain of restaurants. You've tried before and you know the competition is fierce, so how do you get that competitive edge? You approach a trade exchange and explain your dilemma to a broker: "This maintenance contract has come up twice in seven years and each time I've missed out on it by a hair. I hear you can help me make them an offer they could never refuse."

Most brokers would have no difficulty in advising you to use a standard industry tactic: use barter to penetrate the market. They would tell you to put in your regular bid of, say, $27,000, plus an *extra* $2,000 making your total bid $29,000. When you present your bid to the chain owner, you will explain that he can pay a portion of your invoice with $6,000 in meal certificates.

It's a deal that is almost guaranteed to go through, even if you are $2,000 or $3,000 above your nearest competitor. Why? Because most restaurants operate on a two-thirds markup for their meals. That means that $6,000 worth of script for meals the owner will be giving you means a cash outlay to him of only $2,000 maximum. Thus, in actual cash, your $29,000 bid will represent a cash outlay to him of only $25,000. For the restaurant, it's barter leverage at work.

If the deal goes through, the trade exchange would buy the meal certificates from you, probably at a 10 percent discount, for $5,400 in trade credits. You can then use the credits within the system to buy products and services you'd normally pay cash for.

Competitor's Bid	
For 40-month painting contract	$27,000
Actual cost to restaurateur of your competitor's bid	$27,000
Your Bid	
For 40-month painting contract	$23,000
Plus $6,000 in meal certificates	$6,000
	29,000
Actual cash cost to restaurateur, of your bid, $23,000, plus $2,000 (calculating 66% markup on certificates)	$25,000

Your Income

Cash from contract	$23,000
Trade credits from sale of meal certificates	$T5,400
($T6,000 minus $T600 for the exchange's commission)	
Total cash and credits	28,400
Minus 5% transaction fee on credit use	270
Net cash plus trade credits	28,130

It's a win-win-win situation for everyone. The restaurateur is getting his maintenance contract for a lower cash price than previously, plus his meal certificates will be bringing people into his restaurant who may be new and potentially valuable customers.

The trade exchange receives its transaction fee, obtains valuable meal certificates it can sell to its members, and has recruited a new and enthusiastic member who will generate transaction commissions over the years.

As the contractor, you have broken into a lucrative market for the cost of the exchange's transaction fees: 5 percent or $T270, and the $T600 discounted on the meal certificates. However, if you paid attention to the broker's advice and charged $2,000 above your regular contract price, this offsets both the fees and the discount fee, and even gives an extra profit.

INCREMENTAL MARKETING

Such deals are not uncommon in the barter industry, in fact they even have their own name: *incremental marketing*. Simply put, this means increasing your share of the market by offering to take part payment in barter. It's not as hit and miss as it sounds, and most commercial trade exchange brokers can put these types of deals together for new clients. Incremental marketing is a smart and aggressive move for anyone looking to expand in these days of increased competition and decreasing markets.

3

Devaluation and Inflation

The use of trade credits instead of cash has been known to give barter a reputation as being difficult to understand and use. People seem to buy and sell on the basis of a few blips on a computer screen with nothing to back them up other than the reputation of the trade exchange and its owners. Does this mean that trade credits are worthless figments of the imagination? Not at all. As long as other members will accept trade credits as payment in exchange for goods or services, they have value. Like any other currency, including the U.S. dollar, trade credits are worth exactly *what they will buy.*

Trade dollars get their value in precisely the same way as any monetary unit: by being accepted in exchange for goods and services. If $T10 will buy you a $10 meal, then there's no reason to believe that the trade dollar isn't worth precisely the same as cash itself. As long as the restaurant owner continues to give you a $10 meal for $T10, you can assume that one trade dollar is equivalent to one dollar cash. And the owner will continue to accept your trade dollars as long as he knows he can exchange them for $10 worth of electrical work or carpet cleaning or bookkeeping, or whatever other service he may need.

RELATIVE VALUES OF TRADE DOLLARS

The real world, of course, sometimes operates below par. You can legitimately expect to find barter leverage in just about any barter transaction, but it doesn't always happen. The trade credits of some trade exchanges are either worthless or significantly devalued in relationship both to the credits of other exchanges and cash itself.

A quick check of the prices charged within an exchange will soon show if devaluation is a problem. For instance, you may find that, in comparison with other exchanges, the prices have been deliberately inflated. Paint costs twice as much with trade credits as on the open market; a bookkeeper demands three times as many trade credits as cash dollars. These types of differentials between normal market value and those within the trade exchange show that the trade credit is significantly devalued. If this is the case, it can soon wipe out any possible leverage advantage, and a trade dollar from this exchange can cost you more than its cash equivalent.

For instance, suppose you have a model car that cost you $1,000 to build. You sell it within the exchange for $T2,000 which means that each trade dollar has cost you 50 cents to get—$T1,000 has only cost you $500. It's good barter leverage, but if a $500 set of skis cost you $T2,000 within the exchange, then this means that you've swapped a model car worth $1,000 for a set of skis worth only $500. If a trade credit becomes devalued like this it can pose as great a problem in the barter industry as a devalued national currency in the world market.

THE ROOTS OF DEVALUATION

It's pointless to deny the widespread perception that trade credits are not as valuable as real money. But if this concept becomes rooted in the minds of trade exchange members, it can eventually cause a major problem: discounting. If a member thinks that his/her trade dollar is inferior to cash, then there is an automatic tendency to devalue it in any deal. For instance, a member may offer to work for $5 cash or $T10, or offer a product for $30 cash or $T50.

Within exchanges, discounting problems arise when members stop believing that $T10 is the same value as $10. This can happen for any number of reasons. Members may feel they can't find the product or service they want within the system, in which case the credits become worthless to them. Others feel that because they are working for "play" money, then it's okay to skimp on the job or give less than the best product. The client feels ripped off and believes that a job done for trade credits is not equal to one done for cash. It's an insidious trend, which leads to the downfall of exchanges. Once established, the effects of this perception are identical to those that happen when a country loses faith in its currency: rapid, uncontrolled price inflation leading to an eventual abandonment of the currency itself.

Many reasons contribute to trade credit suddenly being devalued within its system, but the only remedy comes from within the exchange itself. Clients usually join an exchange in good faith, so if they start to discount their own currency, it's usually because the exchange is not providing what they want. Ray Bastarache, president of Barter Network Inc. and 1994 president of IRTA, one of the industry's two professional associations, frankly admits that exchanges that can't maintain the value of their trade credits are a drag on the industry's growth.

"Any exchange that allows clients to discount trade credits is not only putting itself in jeopardy, but reinforcing the public perception that barter is somehow fringe marketplace. It's only when an exchange insists that credits be treated with as much respect as cash deposits that it can claim to be a part of the mainstream industry trend."

THE FLUCTUATING VALUE OF THE TRADE CREDIT

Psychological devaluation tends to feed on itself, driving prices upward as the value of the money plummets downward and creating imbalances in the value of trade credits. Although the barter industry as a whole uses the terms *trade credits* or *trade dollars*, the trade credits from one exchange are not necessarily the same value as those from another. How much, then, is a trade credit really worth? The answer: *whatever it will buy within the exchange that issued it.*

As an example, if a restaurateur suddenly demanded $T15 for a $10 meal, you could rightly think, "My trade dollar has been devalued." So, the next time someone wants you to work for trade dollars, you will raise your rates accordingly. Instead of pegging your charges to your open market rates, you'll charge fifteen trade dollars or ten dollars cash.

When this type of devaluation is widespread throughout a trade exchange it has the effect of depressing the value of its trade credits in relationship to other exchanges. Suppose a restaurant belongs to both Exchange A and Exchange B. The restaurateur gets excellent service and products for Exchange A's trade credits and accepts them on par with a cash dollar. The restaurateur has found that Exchange B has a comparatively small selection and its trade dollar will buy service and product worth only 50 cents on the open market or at Exchange A. In the restaurateur's estimation, the trade dollar of Exchange B is worth half as much as a trade credit of Exchange A.

PURCHASING POWER

Trade dollars from different exchanges do not necessarily have equal purchasing power. Each trade exchange is essentially a private world issuing its own currency to its own people, and the chances for financial mishandling are as real for any other closed financial system. Theoretically, each trade dollar issued by the American trade exchange is worth one dollar U.S., regardless of which exchange is talking. In reality, the actual *purchasing power* of a trade credit from Exchange A can be as much as 10 times less than a trade credit issued by Exchange B. In more formal terms, trade credits from Exchange A are devalued 10:1 to those from Exchange B. There is no established value for a "trade credit." It is a misnomer, a catchall term used to describe something that can vary in value from one U.S. dollar to zero.

An analogy to the variable value of trade credits is the relationship of different currencies in Europe. A push to blend all these currencies together and create one currency for the whole of Europe runs into constant

difficulties, the major one being that none of the currencies have equal *buying power.* Internationally, the German mark is favored over the French franc and the
Italian lira. The British pound is stronger than the
Belgian franc and the lira but not as strong as the mark.

This rating of currency strength is based on what the
money can buy *in its own country,* either in goods,
investments, interest payments, real estate, and so on.
For instance, $1000 in German marks is stronger than
$1,000 in Italian lira because from an international
perspective Germany is perceived as having more desirable goods and services than Italy. One money trader put
it this way: "When you talk of Italian lira, you're talking
olive oil, sports cars, and strikes. If you talk about the
German mark, you're talking steel, hard work, and
technical genius. It may be an unfair perception, but it's
what the money world believes."

Within the barter world, trade credits are rated in
much the same manner. Exchange B is perceived by the
rest of the industry as having a weaker trade credit than
Exchange A. The reason? Like Italy, Exchange B doesn't
have the goods and services to back up its currency.
Instead of being able to buy $1 of goods with $T1, you
need $T10, or maybe you can't buy what you want at any
price. The trade credits of an exchange like this will be
devalued to the point of worthlessness, and one of the
worst traps for a prospective barterer to fall into is to join
an exchange that has a devalued currency.

DISPARITY OF TRADE DOLLAR VALUES

Devaluation can be handled successfully on an individual trade exchange basis, provided it is spotted
early enough and the operator knows what to do. But

trade credit disparity between exchanges continues to dog the industry. In the United States, with over 450 trade exchanges, the lack of an even playing field can often be seen in how individual members try to barter their credits between exchanges. I know a man from Seattle who tried to trade $T2,600 from Exchange B for $T600 from Exchange A. He was so discouraged in his efforts to find something to spend his credits on in Exchange B that he was willing to cut his losses and swap for the currency of a stronger exchange. I told him he was a one-man devaluation team.

"Oh no," he replied, "there's lots of us trying to do it."

Trade credit disparity also shows up in intercity trading, the industry's own version of economic unity. The general concept is to link separate trade exchanges across the country. In theory, this will give all members better access to a wider variety of services, making for a happier and stronger network. In practice, such networks often highlight the differences between the soundness of exchanges and the strengths of their respective trade credits and lead to wrangling over price hikes, lack of desirable services and products, and tardy delivery.

REASONS FOR DEVALUATION

One reason why trade credits become devalued can be because an exchange doesn't just offer enough diversity or choice of services and product. Under such circumstances there is a tendency for members to bid against each other in an attempt to buy what is being offered. For instance, the sole printer in one exchange found himself so swamped with offers of work from other members that he refused to do any more printing on barter. Several members then offered to pay him double his usual rates if he would do their work for trade credits, thereby devaluing their own credits by 50 percent.

Another reason for devaluation can be when members stop actively looking for ways to spend their trade credits. Without a keen consumer market, trading can slow down so much that the members lose confidence in the entire process.

Members can be discouraged about spending their trade credits because there is little choice or simply because they see the exchange more as a place to sell rather than trade. If a trade exchange doesn't educate new members properly there is a danger they will assume the exchange is a place to primarily dispose of goods and services. Barter doesn't work as a one-way street. If members only try to sell their goods and services to one another, they are working against the entire concept of the system. Bartering has to be a two-way transaction, and it works best when all the participants are just as keen to *consume* products and services as they are to provide them.

But whether their reason is a lack of choice or a misunderstanding of barter, members who have glutted accounts of trade credits eventually start to demand cash instead of trade for their services or products, or they stop trading altogether. After all, with an account balance of $T20,000 which you are not going to spend, why accumulate more? Glutted accounts lead to slow-down in trade, a dangerous tendency that responsible trade exchange operators try to avoid by continuous scanning of account balances. If they feel something's amiss, they'll contact the client and try to find out if they can help.

One creative response involved a dentist's account that had accumulated over $T100,000. A developer had run out of funds to finish an office block conversion and needed about $100,000 to complete the job. He had used up his usual financing sources, so he turned to a trade exchange for help. The exchange searched their accounts for large accumulations of trade credits and found the dentist. It contacted the dentist, who financed the remaining renovations with his trade credits, which paid not only for trades and labor but most of the materials as well. In return, the dentist took a six-year, rent-free lease on the block with exceptional renewal terms.

The dentist had actually stopped trading in the exchange several months earlier, but unlike many members who accumulate massive trade credit balances he hadn't become disillusioned with barter. He admitted he'd been too busy to think about how to spend them. But after the transaction that put him into his new office suite, he became just as eager as ever to take on barter patients.

CASH BLENDS

Devaluation also occurs when you start insisting on a "blend" of trade dollars and cash. For instance, instead of asking for $T15 an hour, you may quote your hourly rate as $5 cash plus $10 trade.

Asking for part cash in a trade transaction is generally discouraged by any commercial trade exchange that has the resources to enforce it. Their reasoning is simple: the clients who demand part cash for their product or services usually want full trade when it comes to buying, and this is regarded as an unfair attitude. They also believe that uncontrolled cash blends are a quick road to large-scale lack of confidence among the members and lead inevitably to devaluation.

However, cash blends cannot be avoided, particularly when a client has a large cash investment in the product, such as an automobile agency. If the client can make a good case for demanding a cash blend in his/her transactions, some commercial trade exchanges compromise by saying that you "buy as you sell"; if you sell your product or service with a 50–50 blend, you can only buy from the system with 50 percent cash and 50 percent credits. Other exchanges would rather lose clients than compromise and refuse to have anything to do with cash blends, insisting that members only trade at 100 percent credit.

Of course, cash blends will occur in the industry whether the head office likes them or not. Cash blends are even insisted on by the seller when the sale is dependent on an additional cash outlay. For instance, with a time-sensitive product or service such as an empty hairdresser's chair or an empty hotel room, the cash outlay is fixed whether the owner likes it or not. To ask for a cash blend is unreasonable; the owner should be glad to turn the loss into trade credits that can be used. If, however, a retail store is asked by a customer to bring in a product specifically for barter, then it is clear that an additional cash outlay is involved and there's no reason why you shouldn't pay a portion in cash. As an example, a clothing store is asked by a barter customer to bring in a $100 jacket. The wholesale cost to the store is $40, and the final cost to the barterer is a blend of $40 cash plus $T60.

Cash blends only work when the markup is high and trade credits can be used for a significant portion of the purchase. Firms that provide products with a low markup (food stuffs, for example), are rarely found in commercial trade exchanges because the additional work of dealing with barterers and trade credits is not worthwhile. Similarly, firms that offer a mixture of low-and high-markup product will often offer only the high-markup products on barter.

CASH BLEND ADVANTAGES

Cash blends were more accepted in the earlier days of the barter industry. Every barter transaction has certain hard costs; even an apparent service-to-service trade, such as between a hairdresser and a carpenter, carries significant hard costs in taxes, rent, tools, power, and so on.

John, a Minneapolis tire store owner, used a cash percentage and barter to keep himself afloat during an economic downturn in the early 1980s. His markup on tires was about 80 percent, but times were tough and the competition was tougher, so soon there was a price war all over the city. John quickly saw that following the price slashing of his competition was a quick way to ruin. He also realized the advantages of joining a barter network, where he offered the membership $50 tires for only $25—far lower than any of his competitors—plus 25 trade credits. For two years, until the economy improved, trade credits paid for his family's dental work, eating out, two rentals of a summer cottage, repairs and painting of his store, bookkeeping, printing, clothing, a pickup truck, and one year's membership in a health club. Non-barter sales gave him enough cash to pay his hard currency expenses such as rent, phone, heating, inventory, and wages. John estimated that barter brought him an additional $30,000 to $40,000 of luxuries and necessities and possibly saved his business.

Did he lose anything by selling tires slightly below his own cost? He doesn't think so: "Barter customers came because I was in the network. They needed tires and I was willing to take their barter credits. When people can cut a deal they can live with, brand-name loyalty and everything else goes out the window. Of course, some of the barter members may have come to me in the normal course of business, but it's unlikely. They came because I was dealing their type of deal.

"Without barter, those two years would have been just a dull grinding, penny-pinching memory. As it was, struggling to make ends meet in the business hardly affected our living standard at all."

John's system of openly using cash blends is more unusual these days. Some exchanges have developed systems that allow cash blends without running the risk of rampant devaluation of their trade credits, but uncontrolled cash blends almost inevitably lead to devaluation and closure. As one exchange owner pointed out, while John's experience with cash blends was favorable, it didn't stop that particular exchange from folding after just three years of operation.

Although not an infallible guide, cash blends and a tendency toward devaluation can often be spotted in an exchange's monthly bulletin. The less confidence members have in the system, the more cash is demanded as part of the total price, or, when trade units are accepted, the price is grossly inflated.

One recent trade exchange bulletin offered the services of a lawyer for $50 plus $T10 and hour, a price structure that indicates the lawyer is using trade dollars as an incentive rather than a genuine trade. In the same publication, a chesterfield sofa was being advertised for $200 or $T600.

CROOKS

Not all devaluation occurs because of disgruntled or misinformed members. The most damaging cause of currency failure is when trade credits lose their value because of deliberate manipulation by the management. The exchange's operators issue so many trade credits that it has the same effect as unleashing the printing presses in prewar Germany—with marks flooding the economy, the money became worthless.

Flooding a commercial trade exchange with too many trade credits is known as *credit inflation*: more money is available than goods to be bought.

Large accumulations of unspendable trade credits can occur because of poor bookkeeping and accounting. For instance, when commercial trade exchanges trade with one another, it's important that each has sufficient product and services to back its credits. If Exchange A has only a small selection but buys extensively from Exchange B, it is possible that Exchange B may finish up with trade credits that cannot be spent.

Monetary inflation can happen through bookkeeping error but mostly occurs because of one simple motive: greed. Although trade exchange operators coyly call themselves "third-party recordkeepers," in reality they not only record transactions between members but issue lines of credit, charge interest, and generally act like miniature, self-regulating banks.

When a trade exchange issues a line of credit to a customer it does not lend out trade credits it already has. Instead it simply opens a fresh issuance of trade dollars, which it then lends to the borrower. These trade dollars are over and above the one already in circulation: in short, the trade exchange has created them out of nothing. Indeed, if one were to refer back to the 1800s when American banks printed their own notes to be loaned out at interest, we could justifiably say that trade exchanges are operating in an identical fashion—and with all the inherent dangers.

Most of the early banks never made it into the twentieth century because of their tendency to print and loan out more bills than their area could support. The same possibility of issuing more trade credits than the system can handle is inherent in the modern trade exchange. The more loans a commercial trade exchange can make, the larger its profits in interest payments. There are few safeguards to prevent trade exchange owners from issuing as many trade credits as they like, and some have fallen for the temptation.

The technical details are easy to understand. Charles, a trade exchange client, asks the exchange for a line of credit of $T10,000 for a printing job he needs to have done. The agreement is that Charles will pay $1,000 cash as front-loaded "interest" on the trade credits he is about to borrow. However, "borrow" is a euphemistic term, since the exchange doesn't need to have $T10,000 on hand to lend. Instead, the operator merely opens a credit/debit account for Charles and credits him with $T10,000, virtually creating the trade credits with a pen stroke.

Charles now has $T10,000 credit and the exchange has $1,000 cash for the service. This is fairly standard practice in the industry and works fine just as long as the operator keeps his loans in check. However, even in the earliest days of the industry some trade exchange operators saw that overissuance of loans of trade credits could be a lucrative business. Charging a modest 10 percent interest on the loan (payable in cash) operators could reap huge profits until the exchange collapsed under the weight of worthless credits. At such times they'd merely close their doors and reopen elsewhere.

Being a client in an exchange that is spending itself into oblivion through monetary inflation is a frustrating experience. Everyone is trying to buy from you and no one wants to sell. Everyone has too many trade credits, and they'll pay any ridiculous price to get something tangible in return.

One embittered ex-member who runs a printing business described the scenario: "It seemed that everyone was phoning for me to do printing for trade—far more trade business than I could ever get back from the system. It didn't take long to realize there were so many loose trade credits floating around that they were virtually worthless. At one point I was offered $T5,000 for $2,000 worth of printing. With hindsight I now understand how that member was still getting himself a deal. He'd paid $500 cash for the loan of those $T5,000. If I had done the printing for him, he'd have simply walked on the debt to the exchange. He'd have paid only $500 cash for $2,000 worth of printing, and I would have been stuck with worthless trade credits. I still believe in barter, but I'll be a lot more careful with the next exchange I join."

DEFICIT SPENDING

Unchecked monetary inflation can soon reduce client confidence in the trade credit and lead to massive devaluation and collapse. But even more damage to an exchange and to the reputation of the barter industry can happen when operators extend unsecured loans to themselves. This is known as *deficit spending*. The profit is made not in interest charges but in buying product with trade credits and reselling it in the cash market-place. Deficit spending was a part of the barter scene from practically its beginnings. Exchange A's owner would see that a member of the exchange was offering a piece of real estate for trade dollars. Exchange A's owner would then issue a line of credit to him/herself to purchase it. Since the central control of all trade credits is in the hands of the exchange owner, it was easy to hide the transaction so that the owner was not obligated to pay back the credits he had "borrowed" from the exchange. As a result, he became the owner of property bought with money he created himself.

The problems created by deficit spending are both technical and moral. Technically, deficit spending results in rapid inflation and devaluation of an exchange's trade credits. Because the owner does not create a corresponding debit to match the credits he has created, the excess credits are released into the general circulation of the exchange creating a monetary inflation of their own.

The moral question is whether an owner should be able to use his/her control of the issuance of trade credits to bypass the necessity to pay back loans to the system. The dilemma has been faced and solved in numerous other alternative money situations—poker chips, for instance. The owner of the firm that makes poker chips is obviously not supposed to pocket a few for his own use at the tables. If he uses them to play, then he should have an investment in them he can lose. In the same way, an exchange owner should be required to repay any trade credits issued to her/himself.

SAFEGUARDS AGAINST DEFICIT SPENDING

The technical mechanisms that make deficit spending possible are still in place. It is not illegal for commercial trade exchange owners to make loans of trade credits to themselves, though it may be illegal for them not to repay the loans. In *Wright v. IRS U.S. Tax Court*, an attorney for the government noted in a stipulated judgment that deficit spending in which the credits are not repaid through legitimate channels could be construed as theft of goods.

Over the past few years a number of things have happened to make deficit spending even less appealing and more risky. Undoubtedly the most effective deterrent was the decision by the IRS that unsecured loans by owners to themselves are taxable income.

This federal decision coincided with the introduction in 1984 of IRS form 1099b, which became mandatory reporting for every client within a trade exchange, including the owners. Improper reporting was hit with a $50 fine for every transaction involved. Suddenly the deficit spenders found out they were risking not only the wrath of their clients but that of the IRS.

AVOIDING TROUBLED EXCHANGES

Today, bad management can still result in an exchange issuing more credits than can reasonably be absorbed by its clients. It's easy to spot and avoid exchanges that are having this type of problem by checking for obvious signs of devaluation. An even greater assurance that an exchange is not deficit spending or creating unchecked monetary inflation is when it can produce a reputable annual audit, open to the public. As the barter industry continues to grow, such an audit is becoming standard practice, particularly for the larger exchanges.

FRANCHISES

Apart from interest on monetary inflation and deficit spending, another source of wealth for barter crooks was once selling franchises. An operator would put together a fancy package and convince naive buyers to part with $15,000 to $40,000 for a system to "print your own money." Some of the new exchange owners did just that and acquired millions of dollars' worth of product before quietly slipping away.

Others hung in and tried to stick by the original intent of barter, servicing their clients and making their profits from transaction fees. However, without adequate training and usually undercapitalized, the majority either walked away or closed their doors. But a few managed to learn enough of their new business to stay and become major players in today's barter world.

Ray Bastarache of B.N.I. has a perspective on the problems caused by unethical operators. "The barter industry has consistently asked the government for the power to deal with unethical practices and we believe our time is near. All we need is for the government and public to become more aware of the value of the barter industry and its potential for leading a marketplace revival in America. When that happens, we'll get the legislation that's necessary. In the meantime, we'll rely on client education and pressure from our national organizations to keep the situation in check."

Today's successes overshadow any contemporary

problems within the industry, so it's not difficult to agree with optimistic views of the future. One merely has to look at the state of the barter industry just a few years ago to realize that the move to establish it as an ethical business is no mere window dressing. Unethical operators still exist, the buyer still has to beware, but by and large barter is moving rapidly from fringe to mainstream marketplace. Within the next few years, we'll see a nationally recognized value for the trade credit and insurance against losses from the collapse of individual exchanges.

4

Choosing an Exchange

Not counting the highly individualized one-on-one firms, there are five different broad categories of bartering from which to choose, each offering a completely different function: commercial trade exchanges, full service exchanges, corporate trade exchanges, countertrade firms, and UltraTrade. There's no doubt that joining a healthy trade exchange can be of enormous benefit. Whether you're McDonnell Douglas looking to save $16 million on redundant fasteners or Herb Maddock taking his family out to California for the weekend, barter works.

DEFINING YOUR BARTER NEEDS

Corporate Trade Exchanges

Barter needs fall into five broad categories. First, there is the need to move large volumes of distressed inventory. For this, you will need either a corporate trade exchange or a full service exchange. The difference between the two is a matter of volume and product. Full service exchanges tend toward moving boutique and other smaller inventories. A corporate trade exchange is geared to larger volumes and greater variety of product. As a rough guide, if your inventory has a wholesale value of less than $200,000, you should probably be looking at a full service exchange. Anything larger will usually go through a corporate trade exchange. Both corporate and full service exchanges can be contacted through the International Reciprocal Trade Association which represents both commercial trade exchanges and exchanges dealing in corporate trading. A list of their members can be found at the end of this book.

A corporate trade exchange deals in big-ticket individual transactions. You are really dealing with professional brokers rather than joining a barter network. Choosing a corporate trade exchange is basically a matter of references, research, and gut instinct. You are going to have to place a lot of trust in the firm of your choice and the best, although not infallible procedure, is talking to satisfied clients. You should also put in a lot of time making sure you understand precisely the steps that are going to be taken and who is responsible.

ULTRATRADE

The second category of barter need is the large-scale barter of excess production on a regular basis offered by UltraTrade. The management of UltraTrade takes pains to distance themselves from being classified as an outlet for distressed inventory and lay emphasis on their program's ability to utilize underused production capacity. They welcome the opportunity to fulfill the barter needs of the corporation interested in ongoing barter of its own production for other product.

UltraTrade is also a member of IRTA. Its management offices are Advanced Artificial Intelligence Systems, in Richardson, Texas.

COUNTERTRADE FIRMS

The third category is if you're looking for a cost-effective way to open or expand an international market. Countertrade firms specialize in taking the legwork out of international trading and also provide a system of minimum risk.

If you're interested in countertrade, then you'll approach either Dan West at the American Countertrade Association in St. Louis or someone like Jay Marshall at Commerce Exchange International in Albany, New York. If you want the broadest of choices, Michael Morrison at Countertrade Outlook in Fairfield Station, Virginia, can sell you a directory of countertraders across the country or even internationally.

COMMERCIAL TRADE EXCHANGES

Finally there are the barter needs of the businessperson who wants to barter for both business and personal products and services. This category encompasses just about every independent business from hairdressing salons to car rental agencies. Their needs are met by the hundreds of commercial trade exchanges across the continent.

Commercial trade exchanges must offer two key ingredients: diversity and activity. Checking the diversity of services and products will tell you if the commercial exchange can meet your specific needs. You can find out by asking some commonsense questions, the first asking to see a current client directory or something that shows the client base. The main thing to look for is if the present client base has the services and products you normally use. And what about geographical representation? If you've got a specific shopping list you're hoping to fill, make sure you can do it without driving all over the state.

What do you spend your money on? What does your firm spend money on, and in what amounts? If you could find a supplier for cut flowers, how much cash would that save you over the year? (One restaurateur used to spend $6,000 annually on flowers for his tables; he now trades for them.) Needless to say, these questions are best asked before you look at the directory. One frustrated client said, "When I saw all those services and products in the directory, I got so flustered I figured there must be something here that I need. After I joined, I found that nothing offered came anywhere close to my life-style or business requirements. It was really disappointing, but it was my own fault for not knowing my needs better."

Checking on the Competition

While you're browsing through the directory, it would also be wise to check out how much competition you can expect from other clients. If you're going to become the tenth hardware store offering free screen door installation, maybe this exchange isn't for you. Some exchanges run computer models to give you instantaneous access to what sort of competition may be in your area; others simply expect you to find out yourself. However, sheer numbers of competitors can be misleading. Some services, such as printers, are heavily used in an exchange and several can survive in a small area. Other services are less needed by exchange clients, and even two in an exchange may be one too many.

VITALITY—A KEY FACTOR

After satisfying yourself that the client base will meet your needs, the next thing to find out is if the exchange is *vital;* that is, are the members actively trading with one another? The membership directory will give you an idea of the size of the client base and the mix of services and products, but it can't tell you which clients are still active traders or who have simply dropped out. It may be that the dentist is no longer accepting trade credits and the service station is demanding 90 percent cash. Trade exchanges are under no obligation to purge their directories, and for an exchange in trouble, it's much too tempting to inflate the client list by leaving on people who have dropped out.

The simplest way to check on the vitality of the exchange is from the clients themselves. Call some from out of the directory. Ask their views of the trade exchange and tell them you're thinking of joining and would like to assess the present state of trading among the membership.

"Are you still trading? Do you accept 100 percent trade credits? Are you satisfied with the operations? Are you having trouble with other members?"

You might also ask if your own business would be welcome. "Do you ever use my type of business?"

Such questions will soon provide you with answers to whether the exchange can provide the services and products you could use and if there is an opening for your type of business within the system. You can also ask questions about the stability and trading practices of the exchange itself, particularly in respect to its policy on deficit spending.

Don't be surprised if the questions aren't all coming from you and if the exchange doesn't seem to be falling over itself to get your business. Established exchanges are as much concerned with your suitability as a client as you are about their suitability for you. You will probably be talking to a broker, someone who will be trying to assess if the exchange needs your services or product and whether you really understand the concept of a commercial trade exchange. Bay Area Barter Exchange insists that a broker and prospective client talk for at least an hour before any decision is made about membership.

YOUR COMMITMENT

Finally, regardless of how impressed you may be with your initial contact, take lots of time to read carefully the small print of your contract and understand it in terms of cash and personal commitment. Apart from enrollment fees, you should be looking out for monthly fees, penalties for nonpayment of transaction fees, and any other fees the exchange might claim. In most cases, these additional fees are reasonable charges. However, all commercial trade exchanges are in the business to make money, and even some of the largest ones are sometimes accused of nickeling and dime-ing their clients. Check with some of the other members to find out the general reputation of the exchange in this area before you sign.

FULL SERVICE EXCHANGES

A full service exchange is a commercial trade exchange that offers a wider range of services to its members. It is bigger and more complicated in its structure than a commercial exchange, but there is no difference in how you make your assessment of one or the other. As with all financial institutions, beyond an obvious lower limit, size and image are not criteria for judgment. Once an exchange has its critical mass of clients established, the size and direction of growth, whether or not to stay as a commercial trade exchange or to expand into full service, is all a matter of personal choice of the owner.

For instance, not all exchanges have grown to the size where they can afford or even want high-tech marketing techniques. Some exchanges are as laid back as a Mississippi weekend, but that doesn't mean they won't give good service or that they won't suit your needs. There are Commercial trade exchanges which have expanded into national networks, with a huge number of clients, but if your business is strictly local, having five thousand potential customers on the other side of the continent may not be much help. If, however, you are seeking to offer accommodations at your motel, then it makes sense to find an exchange that has connections all across the nation. The ultimate test as to whether or not an exchange is for you is not its size but its ability to satisfy your needs.

FINDING A COMMERCIAL OR FULL SERVICE TRADE EX-CHANGE

It's not difficult to find a commercial trade exchange or a broker's office near you. Trade exchanges are keen to have their name in the public eye, and once you start looking, they become obvious. If you can't find an ex-change through the Yellow Pages or your local Chamber of Commerce or simply by asking other businesses in the neighborhood, then you can contact either the International Reciprocal Trade Association (IRTA) in Great Falls, Virginia, or the National Association of Trade Exchanges (NATE) for a list of their members. NATE doesn't have a set of offices; its address moves with each new president. The 1994 offices are with Les French at InterCity Network in Portland, Oregon. Another excellent source of information is Bob Meyer, owner of *Barter News*, in Mission Viejo, California. Consult the list at the end of this book for these addresses and the addresses of the associations.

5

The Commercial Trade Exchange

If you had to define the core of the barter industry, you'd probably point to the commercial trade exchange, the system that allows individuals and companies to trade with one another on an ongoing basis by using trade credits instead of cash. Trade exchanges that run on barter units in place of money are not new; in fact, much of North America was built on the closed barter system of the company store. This simple credit system led the way for the emergence of more specialized barter operations, such as corporate trading and UltraTrade.

In the barter world, commercial trade exchanges claim historical tradition and are undoubtedly the most high profile. They outnumber corporate trade exchanges by a ratio of eight to one, and they cater to the greatest number of clients: over 450 across the nation service an aggregate client base of about 175,000 companies of varying sizes.

Of course there are size differences between the exchanges themselves. The 35 largest commercial trade exchanges handle approximately 50 percent of the estimated $700 million transactions that flow through the system annually. Of the 450 plus exchanges, nearly two hundred are subsidiaries of a formal network of exchanges called *broker networks*. Three major networks are in the United States, and they form the top tier of exchanges.

COMMERCIAL TRADE EXCHANGE SYSTEMS

The heart of the commercial trade exchange is its operating system, its way of handling debits and credits and its method of attracting members. Although operators tend to be fiercely defensive about their own way of doing things, the differences in trade exchange operations are really differences of personalities and sophistication rather than structure. The transactions of the members are still credit and debit operations, and getting new members still calls for good selling and service skills.

With minor differences, trade exchange systems have become standardized across the continent. The basic structure of a barter network is not a complicated affair. A central accounting office keeps track of clients' expenditures and incomes. This is a vital function since it is these accounts that provide the clients with their substitute for cash. Every credit is a representation of money in the client's pocket, while every debit is the same as money spent.

The accounting base is also used to assess transaction fees for the exchange. According to the policy of the exchange, every transaction will generate a fee that has to be paid in cash, either from the seller or both buyer and seller. Finally, the accounts department also has to provide information about every transaction at year's end, both for the clients and for the IRS.

Keeping track is done by a computer database adapted to fit the special operations of each exchange. The software is cheap, but reprogramming and hardware, including backup machines, can be expensive. Today's exchange accounting system can easily cost in excess of $20,000 according to how it's networked.

SERVICING THE CLIENT BASE

Maintenance of the client base is a necessary component of any trade exchange. Once an operator has a critical mass of members, it has to be kept together and trading has to be encouraged. To do this, it's essential that every member knows exactly what every other member is offering in the way of services and product and what his/her trade dollar will buy. This is all done through intercommunication, set up and fostered by the exchange itself.

Most exchanges still put out an annual or biannual directory of members' products and services and usually a monthly bulletin service that lets everyone know who's joined, who's left, and special deals available. However, it may be that new technology will make the directory and even the bulletin things of the past, since the fax machine is introducing a whole new dimension into the industry's way of servicing clients. One development is Marketfax, which Mark Tracy, 1993 president of NATE and owner of American Commerce Exchange in Toluca Lake, California, explains this way: "A client faxes a request for a certain service or product and we fax him or her back a complete up-to-date list of what's available not only in our exchange, but in all other subscribing exchanges as well. For instance, if one of my clients wants accommodations in Boston, we can instantly access our reciprocal exchange in Boston and have a list of what's available to my client in the same day."

For local business, some exchanges are now replacing the yearly directory with telephone systems similar to Chicago Barter Corp's Dectalk. You phone in and follow the instructions: "PRESS ONE FOR PRODUCTS, PRESS TWO FOR SERVICES, PRESS 18 FOR FLORISTS, 25 FOR AUTO GLASS . . . it's a talking Yellow Pages that's being continually updated.

These systems also let you check up on the credit rating of a potential buyer and give your own account balance at any time of the day or night.

THE CLOSED EXCHANGE

Member directories, talking or otherwise, are not a part of the "closed exchange" where a client approaches other clients through the exchange itself. It works this way: you have a small radio and TV repair shop, an ideal business for trade because of the high proportion of labor involved. You decide to join Exchange XYZ, hoping to access some sports equipment for the family, especially ski equipment. The owner of the exchange has assured you that he has sports suppliers as clients and that you'll have no difficulty filling your shopping list.

In most trade exchanges new members are given a directory of all the products and services available, but in a closed exchange like XYZ, members notify the exchange center about what they are looking for, then wait for the center to find it. The rationale behind the closed exchange is that it has more immediate contact with what has become available. From the exchange's point of

view, a closed system also ensures that it gets its transaction fee; members are not sneaking behind their backs
cutting their own deals.

Many things work against the concept of a closed
exchange. The first is that it shuts down spontaneous
trading, which occurs when people are simply browsing
through a directory—barter's equivalent of impulse buying. Second, it inhibits random contact between clients,
the type of contact that often provides new ideas. Third,
a closed exchange is so blatantly designed for the conve-
nience of the exchange itself that it goes against the first
rule of barter: service your client's needs. It's obvious
why closed exchanges are rapidly fading from the scene.
Trading is prompted by exposure and the exchange
directory that, just like the junk mail flyer, is a constant
incentive to get out and trade. In a closed exchange, the
client not only must develop the need but must think of
the exchange as a place to fill it.

THE BROKER

The crucial staff for any exchange are the brokers,
men and women who sell enrollments and keep continuous tabs on their clients. Many exchanges have in-house
regulations that their brokers must contact high-volume
clients on a regular basis—sometimes as frequently as
once a week—to field possible complaints and inform
them of new opportunities. A good broker keeps his/her
clients' products and services constantly in front of other
clients and seeks deals that may be of interest. It's all
part of the push to encourage members to trade with
each other and nip potential problems in the bud.

THE CONTRACT

Built into the entire concept of a trade exchange is the need to keep a watchful eye on how clients behave with each other. Once a new client has signed on, he or she becomes a member of a club that has a certain set of rules of trade. These rules are put forth in a formal contract; most of them revolving around getting the members to act honestly with each other and with the trade exchange itself. The new client promises to respect the trade credit as legitimate currency, promises to pay the trade exchange its transaction fees, and promises to provide good service or products to other members. One other important agreement is to not make private deals with other members to avoid paying transaction fees. One of the amazing things about trade exchanges is that even without vigilant enforcement, these promises usually work.

INCOME SOURCES

Commercial trade exchanges make money in a variety of ways. Their major source of income is a service fee, which is charged on every transaction—commonly 5 percent to both buyer and seller. This is always a cash charge, payable at month's end. The fundamental success of an exchange therefore rests on its ability to assemble a critical mass of clients who will generate large and continuing transaction fees. Because diversity is a major key to a successful barter network, exchanges strive to bring in a variety of services and products to make membership appealing and worthwhile. If members feel they can access significant products and services for their barter dollars, they're enthusiastic about selling their own services to other system members.

A more recent source of income for many exchanges is the monthly fee for maintaining membership. This can range from $10 a month to $35. Not all exchanges are charging this fee as yet, but there seems to be wider acceptance of it within the industry and it could become a standard before very long.

A downside for barter when working in a depressed economy is that a small business can close its doors, leaving the exchange out of pocket for its fees. Also, a poor economy tempts some clients to dodge paying transaction fees by cutting deals between themselves without notifying the exchange. Others deliberately delay payment until the exchange, in desperation, uses a collection agency.

Collecting transaction fees is still a headache for some exchanges that don't feel big enough or tough enough to enforce rigid collection practices. Today the most successful exchanges insist on a credit card number, which they immediately charge fees to if they aren't paid promptly.

ENROLLMENT FEES

In addition to transaction fees, exchange operators also charge a one-time enrollment fee of about $500. Some systems accept their own trade credits as payment or a mixture of both dollars and credits. Others charge trade dollars for potentially large accounts and cash for accounts that will be dealing with smaller transactions. One large exchange waives the enrollment fee in place of a larger transaction fee. When you sign up, you can either pay an enrollment fee and 5 percent on every transaction or no enrollment fee and 6 percent on everything you buy and sell.

At least two systems charge twice the amount in trade credits as they would for a cash membership. They defend this apparent betrayal of their own system of dealing only in trade dollars with the reasoning that most of the costs involved in getting a new client on line are hard office costs such as wages, rent, and so on.

OTHER INCOME

Apart from monthly charges, transaction fees, and enrollment costs, bigger exchanges have other sources of income. There is, for instance, interest charged on loans of trade credits. Although the industry is experimenting with other ways for members to pay interest charges, usually they are paid in cash, often at open market rates.

Other profits come from the sale of inventory acquired by the exchange either through simple purchase or through more complicated deals, similar to sequential trading. Trade exchanges have begun to look more and more like one-stop shopping centers as they strive for ways to make barter more appealing and diverse. Trade exchanges actively look for special deals for their clients, buying block hotel accommodations or car rental or airplane travel or distressed inventory at discount and selling these to members. The exchanges may approach the vendors themselves or go through intermediary specialists.

Exchanges will directly approach restaurants and hotels in their area and arrange to buy meals and rooms for trade credits. The restaurant gets extra customers and the hotel gets rid of empty rooms in exchange for products and services from the trade exchange clients.

Trade exchanges with a good rapport with exchanges in other cities will often swap hotel bookings in their area for hotel rooms elsewhere. A Dallas exchange might swap hotel rooms based on the assumption that a hotel booking in Dallas is probably more interesting to someone from an exchange in another place than to someone who already lives in Dallas.

Deals for members can be outstanding. Timeshare condos in Mexico, windjammer cruises in the Caribbean, vacation packages in Guatemala, designer jewelry, fur coats, and ski lodge rentals in Colorado are just some of the items that have been offered by exchanges to their members, often on 100 percent trade credits or an attractive blend of cash plus credits. By providing such offerings, the trade exchange benefits in important ways. It reinforces the image that a barter exchange is a good place to find bargains, and it generates trade credits and cash profits for itself.

THE THREE LEVELS OF COMMERCIAL TRADE EXCHANGES

The core operation of all commercial trade exchanges is basically the same, but the ways in which they grow and the ways in which they market themselves can vary dramatically. There are three unofficial tiers of trade exchanges, two of which represent quite different approaches to expansion.

First Level

The lowest tier consists of the "small independents" with a client base of perhaps 20 to 200 members. Another, less flattering title for these operations is often "distressed exchange," because they are usually floundering in a no-man's-land of viability. There's no real cutoff point between a floundering small exchange and a viable one except a feeling that one is "part-time" and sporadic. Within this category of small independent would be franchise operations that were bought several years ago but, through lack of training, support, or simply lack of interest, never managed to grow beyond a certain level. These exchanges often have their own definition about trade credits, and potential clients should perhaps stay potential.

Second Level

The next tier up is the professional full-time exchange that has a solid active base of from 200 to 4,000 or more members. You won't expect to find much variety of products and services within an exchange of only 200 active clients, but they can be helpful, especially if they're trading with other exchanges on a regular basis. Most exchanges that have built a niche in their local marketplace have also got an informal network of *affinity traders* with whom they regularly exchange products and services and help with one another's client needs.

At the top end of the second tier are industry giants, such as TradeAmericanCard of California and Chicago Barter Corp. Both have a client list of over 3,000, which includes professional services, small- and mid-size businesses, plus access to travel and hospitality corporations that make regular offerings of package deals to clients. Most such independent trade exchanges with a large client base are evolving into full service exchanges: part corporate barter, part media agency, part travel agency, part donated goods exchange—a multitude of services they believe will enhance their services to their clients and earn greater profit for themselves. You can expect and you will get a wide variety of goods and services within these exchanges.

The spectrum of products and services available in some systems is so large that an exchange can meet most of its needs directly from its own client base. For instance, Steven White, president of Cascade Trading Association, loves to tell of his 1989 ski trip. His equipment was paid for with trade credits, as were his ski clothes. His accommodations were 100 percent trade credit, and the surgeon who fixed his torn knee was part of the exchange and was also paid in trade dollars, as were the pharmaceutical drugs and hospital!

Within the industry there are probably one hundred exchanges that could be classified as second tier, twenty with client bases of over a thousand and the rest spread out below them. From the smallest to the largest, the second-tier independents have one thing in common: they play in their own backyard, building their clientele inside a limited geographic area and relying on informal networking to gain a wider reach.

Third Level: The Broker Network

Not so the third tier of exchanges: the broker network. The three major players, also known as the "Big Three," in this league are: ITEX Corporation of Portland, Oregon, with approximately sixty locations; BXI (Barter Exchange International) in Burbank, California, with eighty-eight offices from South Carolina to Alaska; and BEI (Barter Exchange Inc.) of Austin, Texas, with over fifty broker outlets. Their structure is one head office with many other subsidiary offices spread throughout the country.

Broker networks really started as franchises networks. At one time barter franchises were being sold at such a fast rate that they threatened to dominate the entire industry. But around the mid-1980s they ran into trouble—quality control. Early sellers of franchises often sold not only the name of the organization and its accounting procedures but the right of the franchise to create its own credits. Indeed, some of the earliest franchises were sold precisely on the idea of "printing your own money." Hog-wild deficit spending, with all its attendant bad press, was often the result. Often the parent organization couldn't or didn't want to oversee what was happening among its kids: it was too busy selling off franchises and pocketing the proceeds.

Today franchising is being replaced by the broker network—one central office supervising and providing central accounting for broker offices across the country. The brokers act independently but use the national network to both sell and access products and services for their clients. Few broker offices are listed with IRTA, but their network's head office will supply local listings.

Franchises and broker offices have quite a few things in common, particularly when they are using a common trade credit. In fact, ITEX built one of the world's largest trade exchanges on the failure of a major franchising operation.

When Barter Systems International ran into serious trouble with its franchise network in the early eighties, a young entrepreneur named Terry Neale created a plan to salvage much of the time and money that had already been invested by franchisees across the nation. Neale would locate a franchise that was in trouble and offer to convert it to become part of the ITEX system, a new network of barter brokers that used a common currency and ran its operations through a central office. The owner would become a broker, paying a percentage of his transaction fees to the head office. ITEX would provide accounting, a single value trade credit (the ITEX dollar), and access to a network of other offices that would, Neale hoped, number in the hundreds.

Unfortunately, Neale's dreams didn't live up to reality. In 1984, after only four years of operation, ITEX was touted by *Barter News* as the fastest growing exchange in the country, with nearly 70 brokers and 15,000 members. It was an impressive start, but in 1992, in an article entitled "ITEX Revisited," Neale spoke of only 55 brokers and 14,000 clients, an almost static situation after ten years of hard work. What went wrong? Industry analysts believe that Neale's broker network formula carries the seeds of its own difficulties. By trying to convert troubled exchanges, Neale also took on their troubled currencies.

An industry observer explains: "It's a bit like trying to convert a hundred different nations to drop their national currencies and deal solely in dollars. There are major problems in deciding who owes what and how much, and what each currency is worth in relation to the next."

There may be other troubles, too. By keeping the old management, ITEX inherited what was often the cause of the problem.

It's an organization that puts on a brave face, which may be true for the head office, but numbers show a different picture for the brokers. In 1992 ITEX posted $100 million in transactions, an impressive figure until one calculates the average return to the 55 brokers within the system: less than $100,000 per office, scarcely enough to pay for rent and phone bills. On the other hand, at 5 percent off the top, the corporate office

ITEX would net itself a cool $5 million. One trade exchange operator speculated the reason why ITEX had 70 brokers in 1984 as compared with 55 in 1992 was that without an adequate return for the majority of brokers, they simply become discouraged and drop out as quickly as others join.

PROS AND CONS OF BROKER NETWORKS

The case for broker networks is a hot subject whenever exchange operators get together. Commercial trade exchanges claim that their structure—solid local trading with an informal network of affinity traders—provides the best products and services to the client. Brokers in networks obviously claim the opposite: that the client can be served best through a formal network stretched out across the country.

A strong advocate for broker networks is Terry Brandfass, who brokers for Barter Exchange (BXI) in Arizona. So far she has built up a client base of over 700, mainly in Tucson but with an expanding clientele in Phoenix.

"I've had a lot of occasions when local exchanges couldn't get product that I could. We have nearly eighty exchanges in our network, which I can call on anytime to meet the needs of my clients. I've got four-color printing from New York and fax machines from L.A. Just maybe some of the large exchanges can compete with me in that type of service, but for the majority of exchanges they are just too small and local."

As for the complaints that weak brokerages and isolated clients merely increase numbers without increasing quality, Brandfass is quick to point out that successful trading depends on the creativity of the client.

A client who understands how to use the system can be anywhere yet still be plugged in to a vast network of supplies.

"Broker networks actually serve the isolated client in ways that a single trade exchange never could. With 1–800 numbers and fax machines, anyone anywhere can put their product or service into the system and make it available for eight thousand people. We see membership for the isolated client as being a potential plus that the average trade exchange just can't provide."

To keep her clients up to date, Terry puts out a quarterly directly plus a weekly "Hot Fax" sheet of new services and products. She also believes in cold calling potential clients, but she does it in a selective way.

"I'm trying to build a base of hotel accommodations in Phoenix, but first I have to have things I can offer them on a regular basis. So at the moment, I'm concentrating on bringing in businesses that a hotel can use."

Unlike Neale, who believes the independent trade exchange will eventually give way to the national network, Brandfass doesn't foresee any dramatic shift in the present mix of the industry. There are so many opportunities that all types of exchanges have room to flourish.

Income Sources for Broker Networks

In the case of the broker networks, income also comes from accounting fees that are charged to the subsidiary broker offices. Each subsidiary pays the head office a fixed percentage, about 5 percent, of its transaction fees in return for centralized accounting and networking. Broker networks also deal in corporate trades and often have impressive inventories of media, travel, and transport.

There is also the initial sale of the territory itself, which is usually paid in cash. It all adds up to one thing: a very lucrative business for the top hierarchy and for people like Brandfass who can make it work.

The Great Debate

The high costs of accounting were the major factor in the emergence of the broker network. A significant advantage is that all accounting is kept in one location, considerably reducing costs.

One person who disagrees with this is Steve Goldbloom, president of Bay Area Barter Exchange. Steve bought a franchise with the massive BX broker network in 1984. A major attraction was the idea that while BX kept the books, he could concentrate on signing up and servicing clients. But within four years he cut ties with the parent company and went independent, relying on his own computer skills and his ability to translate them into servicing his clients.

Because they are spread out across the nation, broker networks are accused of trying to play in everyone's backyard, and there's no doubt this has caused some friction in the industry. The philosophy behind the broker network is geographical expansion, with the belief that the variety and availability of services and products will be greatest if one can select from across the nation. It's a debate that seems never ending and without a real resolution. From the client's perspective, however, it's obvious that the only real criteria for success is if the network or exchange meets his/her needs.

PROFITS

When it comes to actual profit figures, all exchanges are the same: close-mouthed. A few actually plead poverty, while at the same time boasting they are the largest exchange in Wishful County. But in spite of the declarations of "just turning a profit this year," there's little doubt that the business is a profitable one if run with good business sense. Using an average figure of sixteen staff per thousand clients, and discounting extra income from interest charges, etc., it would seem that such an office has the potential to generate around $600,000 to $1 million in gross profits annually. However, if a trade exchange uses its client base as a springboard into the more profitable corporate trading of distressed inventory, the bottom line can be considerably more. Corporate trade profit figures are more closely guarded than trade transactions.

GROWTH PATTERNS

The typical financial growth pattern of a highly profitable exchange seems to be first to develop a solid base of clients trading a high number of transactions then to expand into offering asset recovery or corporate trading for specific, high-profit deals. On the high end of the scale, independent offices which have followed this formula regularly transact $20 million annual volume ($2 million gross profit), while some of the nationwide groups with sixty satellite offices are rumored to have gross barter sales in excess of $100 million.

Obviously the primary goal of the trade exchange is to enroll enough members to take it from just getting by into profitability. It can be a long haul. Commercial trade exchanges that don't widen their scope of trade options must make their money from transaction fees, and it can be quite a struggle to get enough members trading with each other to simply pay for expenses. To give an idea of what this means in terms of effort and investment, one hundred members trading $6,000 each will generate a gross profit to the exchange of a mere $60,000. It's not a fabulous income by any stretch of the imagination, and some offices, even those on broker networks, make even less. An obvious component, therefore, of any exchange is vision. Any operator needs to look into the future and see the type of expansion that is needed to take the exchange into profitability.

Ray Bastarache founded his trade exchange, Barter Network Inc. (B.N.I.) in 1985 using a $3,000 loan that he got from his parents. At 23 he was the youngest independent exchange owner in the country, working out of a 400-square-foot office in the corner of a warehouse in Bridgeport, Connecticut.

Like many exchange operators who started on less than a shoestring, Bastarache had to play every role in the business: receptionist, accounts clerk, and all the roles expected of a broker. Also like many others, he drew his sole inspiration from a belief in barter and the benefits it could bring both to himself and his clients. But after eighteen months of fourteen-hour workdays, he still hadn't reached the critical mass of members that would allow B.N.I. to really take off. Then Paul Nedovich, president of Recreational Marketing Associates, entered the picture. He was building the Eagle's Nest Resort, a summer getaway in central Vermont, and he welcomed the chance to use B.N.I.'s small but solid client list. Bastarache credits Nedovich with being the first notable breakthrough: $600,000 in trade and a major drawing card for new members.

Today, B.N.I. has annual trades of over $10 million on which Bastarache receives a 12.5 percent transaction fee. This is one of the highest transaction fees in the industry but Bastarache claims to be part of a trend, providing higher quality service for which the customer is willing to pay. He is busy introducing new consumer programs that will turn B.N.I. into a true full service exchange. He's moved out of the old office and now operates from a 9,000-square-foot facility in Milford, Connecticut, with a branch office in nearby Hartford. On the way up he's managed to acquire four homes, including one beachfront property on Long Island Sound.

In his spare time, Ray has also managed to collect an impressive array of business awards, some commercial real estate, and a piece of the USBL Skyhawks basketball team. In the barter industry, he's known as one of the bright, new generation that will not only bring expansion to the industry but clear out much of the old image. What is his secret for continuing success? "Servicing clients and having an aggressive, smart staff to help, but most of all the vision to know where you are going."

6

The Corporate Trade Exchange

Corporate trade exchange and commercial trade exchanges may sound similar, but their functions are poles apart. Whereas the commercial trade exchange deals in a continuous flow of goods and services among its clients, the corporate trade exchange specializes in brokering massive, customized trades between two or sometimes three parties.

Corporate barter came into being to fulfill a pressing need in corporate America—getting rid of unwanted inventory without actually giving it away. Unwanted, unused, distressed inventory has always been the bane of the manufacturer, but never so much as in times of economic recession. A sluggish marketplace means that production will invariably catch up with and pass sales, and at that time the warehouses start to fill up with the unwanted and unsalable.

Apart from an economic slowdown, there are lots of other reasons for a manufacturer to suddenly find itself with plenty of its own product on hand. There may have been a style shift in the marketplace, for instance, and an improved model has suddenly caught the attention of the dealers and no one wants the older model anymore. Or what about shifts in fads? Somewhere there must be at least a million hula hoops gathering dust in some forgotten building. Or straight competition can do it. And exclusive territory grabbed by a competitor offering a similar product at a lower price can happen faster than the production line can be closed down.

Whatever the reason, excess inventory is to any corporation like a rock thrown in its path, an obstruction that must be dealt with before regular business can carry on. It bothers the accounts people, the warehouse people, the sales people, and the production people.

Until the mid-1980s, the solutions to excess inventory were few, painful, and usually involved selling everything off at pennies on the dollar. Even if a buyer could be found, a manufacturer had to make sure that his fire sale inventory wasn't going to reappear in his regular distribution territories, where it would compete with existing dealerships.

The people who hate liquidation sales of distressed inventory most are those in the accounts department. Selling $1 million of inventory for $5,000 looks really bad on the books, and if the markdown is especially large, it can jeopardize the entire credibility of the firm.

BARTER'S SOLUTION FOR DISTRESSED INVENTORY

It took a group of specialized barterers to find a solution to the problem of distressed inventory: the invention of corporate trade. The concept was quite simple: swap excess inventory that the firm doesn't want for something the firm does want, such as media and advertising space. For example, a manufacturer of small sailboats finds his market has dried up. He decides to start building cabin cruisers but first he has to liquidate $1 million of inventory. What to do? The barter option is to find someone who wants $1 million in sailboats and who has equipment or services that the manufacturer can use in his new operations. They swap their apples for oranges and everyone is happy.

Of course, when it comes to putting this into practice, the concept is more difficult. Once again we run into the problem of how to find someone who wants a firm's excess inventory and is willing to swap something of value for it. The solution is the third-party broker, the corporate trader who acts as a middleman, who finds the party who wants the inventory and what the party can exchange for it.

PUTTING TOGETHER A CORPORATE TRADE SWAP

The first thing a corporate trader must do is find something that he/she can buy that can be swapped for excess inventory. The product has to be right and the price has to be right, because this is where the trader will make part of his profit. Corporate traders specialize in negotiating deep discount buy options; that is, discounts on prices that have already been discounted. For example, an office furniture supply company may sell a chair for 15 percent below regular retail. A corporate trader will persuade that company to supply the chairs at 25 percent below retail. Traders are successful at these type of negotiations for two reasons: because they're usually talking in large numbers, and they're also talking repeat orders.

Corporate traders also make it their business to

know the state of the nation's warehouses—where distressed or liquidated inventory can be bought for significant savings. In brief, they have the pulse of the discount world and can usually, given time, come up with just about any item below the best price you can find.

Most frequently corporate traders shop for "bulk" media and advertising space. Like hotel rooms and restaurant meals, media and advertising space is *time sensitive:* you can never regain the revenue lost from an empty radio spot or a magazine quarter page for which you couldn't find an advertiser. The corporate trader can usually negotiate favorable terms by promising bulk buys. In effect, what the trader says to the media is: "If I bring in an order for $1 million worth of advertising time, I'd like to be able to buy time for $500,000 cash."

For TV and radio stations and for magazines that are having trouble attracting advertisers, this can be an attractive proposition. Since there is a deadline with all time-sensitive products beyond which there is *no* return at all, it makes sense to give this trader a chance to sell your product in bulk, even if you have to pay him 50 percent commission.

With an agreement from the media in hand, the trader now has something tangible to work with. What he will do is swap the media time, which he has arranged to buy for a 50 percent discount, for its full retail value in excess inventory. For example, if he has arranged to buy $1 million of media time for just $500,000, he will swap that time for $1 million of distressed inventory. Of course, the actual figures and percentages can vary significantly but the general principle does not. The trader "buys" $1 million of inventory for media time for which he has paid only $500,000.

On the books however, the owner of the inventory has basically swapped $1 million of distressed inventory for $1 million of media time. Both the media and the owner of the inventory have benefitted by disposing of unwanted inventory for something of value. The media receives $500,000 and the owner receives a million dollars worth of advertising.

The trader makes his profit in two ways. First, there is a simple broker's commission on the transaction which he has negotiated between the media and the manufacturer. The second profit lies in the distressed inventory itself which the trader acquires for basically nothing but his expertise. The deal starts by the trader using trade credits to "buy" the distressed inventory. However, these trades credits can only be used by the manufacturer to buy media time for the prearranged source: the one that the trader has negotiated for $500,000. Also, these trade credits can only be used with a cash blend. To buy one dollar's worth of advertising, the manufacturer must spend 50 cents cash and 50 cents in trade credits. If the manufacturer wants to buy $1 million of media time with the trade credits, he must spend $500,000 in trade credits plus an outlay to the trader of an additional $500,000 in cash. In effect, this pays the trader for the time which he has prebought from the media in the first place.

EXAMPLE OF CORPORATE TRADING

Say corporate barter group Invenswap Corporation has already negotiated with a group of radio and TV stations to buy media advertising time for 50 cents on the dollar. The buy has to be completed by a certain date, there are restrictions on time slots, and so on. But that's normal for the business, and the president of Invenswap is confident that he can find a deal.

And he does. Beachware Unlimited approaches Invenswap for help in disposing of $1 million worth of windsurfing boards. A design breakthrough has created a new type of board, which has muscled out the old design. Beachware's distributors are returning the old stock and demanding the new, creating an inventory logjam.

Beachware Unlimited is contacting Invenswap because of an ad that Invenswap runs in a local business journal:

WE WILL BUY YOUR EXCESS INVENTORY
AT FULL WHOLESALE PRICE.

Is this possible? Is there an outlet for the old windsurfing boards that Beachware could have overlooked? To the harassed accountants at Beachware, the ad sounds too good to be true. But the head accountant and the general manager set up a meeting with the president of Invenswap. They tell him of their distressed inventory problem and he responds, "With your new line of boards coming out, you'll undoubtedly be looking at a substantial advertising budget to launch the product."

The accountant agrees, in fact Beachware Unlimited has already budgeted a $3 million advertising campaign over the next year in radio, TV, and print. Invenswap's president then explains his corporation and what it does: "What we can do here at Invenswap is take all your distressed inventory off your hands and replace it with the equivalent retail value in advertising. If you give us $1 million in inventory, we will give you $1 million in advertising at competitive prices. We'll need to go over your entire advertising program in detail to make sure we can provide what you want from our media sources, but I am sure we can do it."

THE CORPORATE TRADE EXCHANGE

Now it's the general manager's turn to get nervous. He has to think of his existing distributors and protecting their territories. The last thing he wants to see is his windsurfing boards turn up at half price next to a store where some are still being sold at full price.

"How will you dispose of our inventory?" he asks.

The Invenswap president has already thought of that and gives assurances that the outmoded boards will only be released outside of Beachware's established distribution territories.

A tentative deal is signed and Invenswap consults with Beachware's advertising division to see if it can provide the required media time. Invenswap will also study the distribution of Beachware's territories and decide on a plan for the inventory, which it will soon control. And it will check with its media sources to see if it can buy the time for Beachware at the agreed 50-50 split.

If everything works out, then a deal is struck with Beachware. Invenswap first takes control of Beachware's excess inventory and credits them with $1 million in trade credits. Invenswap then sells the media time which it has negotiated to Beachware at *full retail price;* that is, the price the radio station would normally charge. However, instead of paying in dollars, Beachware will pay Invenswap 50 percent in cash and 50 percent in trade credits. In other words, Beachware will buy $2 million of advertising for just $1 million cash and $1 million worth of excess inventory.

It's a win-win-win situation. The media has sold its advertising, Invenswap has acquired $1 million worth of inventory for brokering the deal and Beachware has successfully swapped its inventory for $1 million in advertising that it would have bought anyway. Beachware's accounting department should be particularly happy—instead of a $1 million loss of inventory, they now have an entry that shows that the excess inventory was used to pay for its full worth in pre-budgeted advertising, $1 million in inventory for $1 million in advertising.

Bookkeeping for Corporate Trade Credits

The book entry system for this type of transaction is really a matter of personal preference. Some firms choose to show the trade credits as income; others prefer to run a dual set of books for the life of the transaction, rounding everything off at the end. Either way, from an auditor's or IRS point of view, the transaction was a barter that has to be recorded as a cash transaction.

Beachware's salespeople will be satisfied for two reasons: there's no more dead stock to worry about, and it's gone to a place where it will never be heard of again. The restrictions on where the windsurfing boards can be sold protect existing distribution networks.

Meanwhile, Invenswap has acquired legal title to $1 million in old-style windsurfing boards. These are payment for the brokering work Invenswap has done between Beachware and the media. At first glance it seems an excessive fee. However, since these boards are outmoded inventory, what are they *really* worth? That all depends on Invenswap's own distribution network. This can include discount stores, mail order houses, other corporate traders, and even overseas distributors. Some possible scenarios for the windsurfing boards could include sale to overseas windsurfing clubs as trainers, sale to a banking institution as a promo giveaway, as prizes in a magazine competition—it all depends on the imagination and connections of the president of Inven-swap and his/her staff.

CORPORATE TRADE PROFITS

Profit figures for corporate barter are a closely guarded secret within the industry, but most speculation is that a corporate barter deal isn't viable without a 10 percent profit potential from sale of the inventory; that is, Invenswap will want to cash out their windsurfing stock at $100,000 minimum.

But just in case they don't manage a profitable cash out, corporate traders also like to build in another source of profit: discounted media time. In our example, the media scrip cost the trader 50 cents, and it was sold to Beachware for 50 cents cash plus 50 cents trade credits. From the trader's point of view it was a neutral deal; all the potential profit was in the windsurfing inventory.

A more likely scenario is that Beachware would be asked to pay 60 cents in cash and 40 cents in inventory for media time. That way the trader makes an up-front profit on the media as well as whatever can be made on the sale of the inventory. In our example, by selling media for 60 cents instead of 50 cents, Invenswap would make an additional $100,000 over and above sale of the inventory.

To an outside observer, the potential profits of cor-porate trading exchanges makes corporate trading sound like a simple and quick way of making money. It may be quick, but it's definitely not simple. First the trader has to gain the attention and the trust of a corporation with a significant inventory problem. He/she then has to persuade that corporation to embark on a course of action that can sound bizarre to the uninitiated and scary to those who don't fully grasp the basic principles. In addition to the normal business stresses, the corporate trader must sell an unusual concept to a skeptical business world.

Then, once the trader has made the deal, the excess inventory must be insured, stored, and eventually sold. It all means time and money and a chance to waste both. To cash out, the inventory might have to be shipped overseas or to another part of the continent, all the time taking care not to infringe on the established territory of the manufacturer and never being sure that the deal may yield nothing more than pennies on the dollar. It all takes special entrepreneurial skills and a belief in the value of what's being offered.

In some cases, the distressed inventory isn't worth much more than liquidation prices, regardless of good intentions. There may be no way in which the trader can cash out easily or profitably. If the return from the cash out looks as if it will be insignificant, he/she will make up the balance by reducing the overall size of the deal. An offer may be made for only half the wholesale value in trade credits, or even less, and the cash percentage needed for a media buy will be raised.

Other times, the inventory will obviously fetch a high cash price in the trader's network and the manufacturer can negotiate to get a part of the final cash out returned. With corporate traders there's no such thing as a standard agreement or contract. Every aspect is up for negotiation.

BARTER AND THE LEASE PRISON

In the past few years, corporate barter has expanded its horizons beyond being primarily an industry that specializes in media swaps; it is now looking for other creative ways to use its skills. For instance, corporate trade is being used to deal with leases that have become too costly to maintain and too costly to break (described in detail in the *New York Times*, 14 February 1993). Lease traps are common in these times when companies are downsizing and relocating in an effort to stay afloat.

In 1988, *Barter News* spotted the trend toward lease bartering and ran an article about how to barter a sublease transaction. In the 1992 fall issue, *Barter News* once again featured the concept, by reprinting *Real Estate Weekly*, "Brokering Sublease Barter Transactions," by Robert Epstein, which describes the "lease prison"—an uncomfortable situation in which a tenant is paying far above market rental in a depressed economy.

The barter solution for the lease prison is technically the same as it is for distressed inventory. A corporate trader will "pay" for the remainder of the lease with trade credits, redeemable through a variety of products and services, on a part-cash, part-credit basis. The trader doesn't actually take title to the lease. Instead, the trader buys with credits the right to sublet the property and keep the income from the new tenant. As has become standard, the most common products on which the tenant may "spend down" credits are advertising services and exposure. The credits are also usually time sensitive; that is, they have to be spent within a certain period of time or else they become invalid.

Occasionally a corporate trader will actually acquire freehold property through barter. The *New York Times* article mentioned above quoted a deal in progress by the veteran corporate trader Tradewell in which a processing plant was traded for credits of advertising exposure. Tradewell then traded the plant to an orange juice concentrate manufacturer and, at the time of writing,

Tradewell was negotiating the trade of the concentrate for an equal value in soft drinks, which will then be cashed out to retailers wrapping up the deal.

Potential Snags

As with inventory swaps, the problem that could arise in barter for real estate is if a corporate trader fails to establish and follow through on the spending of the credits that he/she has issued. For example, a corporate trader offers $500,000 in advertising and $500,000 in hotel accommodations for $1 million of leaseholder's space. The trader then subleases the space to a client for $600,000. (It may seem like a losing situation, but invariably the advertising and accommodations have been bought at wholesale prices, far below the $1 million that the leaseholder has to pay for them.)

The subtenant now settles into his bargain space, but the deal is not really complete until the leaseholder has spent his credits—and this is where problems can occur. If the corporate trader has been negligent in establishing a clearcut deal with both the advertising people and the hotel chain, the leaseholder can find that spending his credits may cost far more than anticipated, or they can't be spent at all. The legal questions that could arise from such a predicament are endless. In particular, what would be the rights of the subtenant?

Corporate Trade Credits: Spend Down Problems

When things don't work out quite so smoothly as they did between Invenswap and Beachware it is often because of misunderstandings about the trade credits that are used to monetize the excess inventory. Although they have the same name, trade credits issued for corporate trade are quite different from the trade credits issued by a commercial trade exchange.

For one thing, commercial trade exchange credits have an unlimited life span; corporate trade credits are usually time sensitive: the client must use them within a certain period or they become worthless. If the spend-down program isn't thought out carefully in advance, a firm could find itself with the daunting task of spending $2 million in trade credits within a few months.

The situation becomes even more stressful when the spend-down requires a substantial cash blend. In our example Beachware had to lay out $1 million in cash in order to use $1 million in trade credits. It often happens that a client may have to lay out a lot more cash than a 50-50 split. In the real world, percentages and discounts vary dramatically according to circumstance and negotiating skills. If the client wants to use trade credits as an assist in buying office furniture, the cash required may be as high as 95 percent. This puts the client's trade credits as a buying incentive into the same class as grocery coupons: it's nice to get change, but it's not worth making a purchase for.

The necessity for a cash blend plus the time sensitivity of the trade credits can easily create a situation where the manufacturer simply doesn't feel able to spend the credits in the time allotted. In effect, the benefits of corporate trading are lost for everyone but the trader, who has managed to get control of the excess inventory for basically nothing. For the trader, even at fire sale prices, a profit can still be made.

Another reason for credits not being spent is that the goods and services promised by the trader are simply not there to be had. It's hard to imagine that a company would give over its excess inventory on the mere promise of a return of equal value, but it happens. The trader may have genuinely thought he had a deal when he really didn't, or he may have used deliberate deceit. Either way, the trade credits aren't spent because the goods or services to spend them on are not there as promised.

The non-use of trade credits is not always the trader's fault. A client may deliberately choose not to spend down trade credits but to keep them as a positive book-keeping statement for the stockholders. Beachware could have claimed the $1 million of trade credits it received as unspent credit with the XYZ media agency, neatly balancing the $1 million in inventory given to Invenswap. When this happens, the manufacturer is placing himself in a tricky position. The IRS taxes any trade credits in the year they are earned, and a manufacturer who corporate trades just for the satisfaction of a clean balance sheet could find it a costly exercise.

Other clients don't spend down their trade credits because they have left the job to others within the organization. This usually occurs when the barter deal is done by accounting and management, and the purchasing department is left out of the discussions. All that purchasing knows is that suddenly $2 million in trade credits has appeared that they are supposed to spend— and they often don't. If left to their own resources they will claim that this new style of shopping is too big a chore, basically sabotaging the process. A solution for this problem is to have every department represented in the negotiations from the start so that everyone knows exactly where the trade credits are to be spent.

And then, of course, there is the change of plans that occurs in every organization and invalidates all the planning that has gone before. Suddenly the advertising budget has shrunk by 50 percent or the agency has decided to take it in a totally new direction. When this happens, the prenegotiated media time suddenly loses its appeal, and with it go the trade credits.

SOLUTIONS

Whoever is to blame, unspent trade credits add up to unhappy clients, and the corporate trade industry has put in a lot of thought on how to correct the situation. One innovative step, which has become an industry standard, was devised by Susan Groenwald, president of Chicago Barter Corp. She developed the *trade purchase request*, a detailed purchase order form that specifies in advance items and vendors who are qualified to fill their needs.

Self-education among traders is also helping. *Barter News* is constantly running articles that exhort traders to "service their clients in terms of their needs." In practical terms, this means sorting reasonable expectations from unreasonable ones and making sure the deal will flow smoothly from beginning to fulfillment. Since no two trades are alike, this presents a constant challenge to the trader to explain precisely what's going on and to educate the client in the niceties of the deal.

Ray Bastarache's B.N.I. is a hybrid operation: a successful trade exchange that has expanded into the corporate barter field. It's been a smooth transition, which he credits to meticulous attention to the client's needs, in particular the way they're going to be fulfilled.

"It's easy to promise the moon and be believed," he says. "Firms with five million dollars in excess inventory are often feeling vulnerable and desperate. But using people's temporary problems is no way to do good business. You have to educate every new client in exactly what you can do and what they can expect. It's not a business that everyone knows about."

FULFILLMENT PROBLEMS

If deals vary dramatically from case to case, so does fulfillment: the performance of the corporate trader. He/she has issued promises to deliver so much advertising or product in return for inventory and cash. Whether or not those promises are fulfilled depends in large part on the integrity of the trader. In the early days it was not unknown for a trader simply to issue trade credits, take control of the inventory, cash it out, and vanish.

One of the latest corporate barter companies to land in fulfillment trouble was the Mediators, a barter media company that McDonnell Douglas chose after an exhaustive search. In September 1991 the Mediators filed for Chapter 11 bankruptcy protection. Media companies that had already provided Mediators' clients with advertising time were owed more than $30 million. The Mediators also owed clients more than $90 million for services and inventory that were promised for trade credits but never fulfilled.

WEAK LINKS IN THE CHAIN

What can break down in corporate trading with such disastrous consequences? Many individual factors could inhibit fulfillment and possibly even abort it, but there seems to be just one central fault: reliance on the trade credit. In the last analysis, corporate trade credits have little intrinsic worth apart from the good intentions of the trader. Unlike the trade credit issued by the commercial trade exchange, which is backed by goods and services, the trade credit of the corporate barter company is at best an

I.O.U. from the company to the client. It does not represent purchasing power that is independent of the corporate trader who issued it. In fact, without the active participation of the trader, the credits are basically worthless.

Unfortunately the industry is reluctant to admit a pretty obvious fact: a corporate trade credit has little more security for the client than a promise of perform. Such a situation, which relies almost entirely on the moral fiber of the trader, is fraught with undesirable possibilities. But it also says a lot for the caliber of those corporate traders who have faithfully stood by their promises and built an entire industry.

PUBLIC FAITH IN CORPORATE BARTER

In spite of periodic scandals, corporate barter has grown into a sober-minded option for inventory-clogged businesses. Yet, it is still a struggle to gain wider acceptance. Ask most corporate traders about the difficulties faced by the industry and you will hear a litany of woes, including the problems created by a checkered past, a periodically troubled present, and an inability to present clearly corporate barter to the business community. This last problem, the lack of a clear image as to what corporate barter does, may have its roots in the presentation of the trade credit as having intrinsic value. Stating that a company can sell its excess inventory for full wholesale is primarily a didactic device to gain a customer's attention, but it does create the expectation of cash value. To be blunt, it may be that corporate traders who are trying to get clients to part with their inventory for trade credits are asking a bit too much trust from their clients.

The unease that seems to lurk within many executives' minds when faced with a corporate barter deal was perfectly summed up by the *New York Times*. After describing Lufthansa's use of a barter company to get rid of an unwanted lease, the article ends: ". . . many executives are uncomfortable trading something as tangible as a building or space for something as intangible as trade credits" (14 February 1993).

It may well be that the credibility dilemma facing the corporate barter industry will not be solved through more education but through the elimination of the trade credits as a significant part of the deal. To any astute observer of the game plan it must be obvious that excess inventory will disappear out of sight and control far more quickly than trade credits. A corporate trader may have a buyer lined up for inventory the next day; the media time to pay for it may not be called on for a year. This time lag creates a confusing picture of what remedies can be effectively taken if the deal goes sour.

One significant part of this confusion is the use of trade credits in exchange for hard inventory; the client company feels, quite rightly, that it is giving up something of value, however small, for promises. The resistance to the growth of corporate trading could lie in precisely this hunch, which cannot be glossed over even with the best of presentations.

So how vital is the trade credit in the performance of a corporate trade? As an accounting device it's absolutely essential, but too often it is presented as having a legitimate purchase value of its own, and this may be where corporate traders are losing credibility.

It's certain that company executives who are potential clients, regardless of how well educated they are in the process, can't see the trade credit in any other light than an accounting device without real objective value. It's a situation that's bound to create unease and will probably stay that way until the industry finds other ways of completing their transactions.

Probably the simplest solution, and certainly the most satisfactory from the client's point of view, would be if legal agreements were established between not only the client and the corporate trader but also between the client and all those involved in final fulfillment, independent of the trader.

By contracting between all the separate parties instead of relying on the trader for fulfillment negotiations, the industry might avoid the periodic collapse of corporate traders and the attendant embarrassment to its collective reputation. It might also find the concept of barter easier to sell to suspicious executives who don't want to part with tangible real estate for intangible promise to fulfill.

SUMMARY OF BENEFITS

In spite of difficulties with image and credibility, the corporate trade industry as a whole is gaining a deserved foothold as a marketplace alternative. Corporate traders have brought very real benefits to American business and public. By wheeling and dealing and a lot of hard work and ingenuity, corporate traders moved an estimated $5 billion plus of excess inventory in 1992. By doing so they managed to keep profits up and losses down for a lot of firms, both small and large, and brought some great buys to the price-conscious public. One trader graphically described his business as "the big laxative. When corporate America can't move anymore because it's bloated with excess inventory, we're the ones who can get it moving." As the economy worsens, corporate trading has no place to go but up.

7

The Full Service Exchange

Speculation about the future of corporate trade exchanges may soon be superfluous as they become replaced by a natural mutation of the commercial trade exchange known as the Full Service Exchange. This exchange has evolved as operators seek to maximize the potential of their organizations by providing an ever widening scope of services. In the mid-1980s it became apparent that an exchange with a solid base of clients could provide better service and fulfillment for a trade of distressed inventory than the larger corporate specialists. It's a logical step for an industry that thrives on greater and greater diversity of products and services.

There are significant differences between how a full service exchange and a corporate trade exchange will deal with distressed inventory. Most corporate traders offer to effect an exchange of media time for inventory, often with a heavy cash blend required. Beachware, for instance, had to spend $1 million in cash in order to spend down $1 million in trade credits.

Two problems that the full service exchange can usually bypass are that of cash blends and the problem of limited choice of products and services. Unlike a corporate trade exchange, a full service exchange can offer access to the entire range of products and services of its client base. And it doesn't cost the trade credit holder any cash to spend down credits.

For example, a manufacturer of plastic products is stuck with a canceled order of 50,000 speciality bottles for a vitamin line that never happened. Instead of going to a corporate trader, he turns to a full service exchange, which buys the inventory using trade credits from its account. The manufacturer can then go on a shopping spree to spend down his credits. By accessing the resources of the associated trade exchange, the manufacturer may choose to spend the credits on a variety of products or services: printing, janitorial services, a morale-building trip to Nevada for top employees, and so on, *often without the outlay of any cash at all.*

This aspect of the full service commercial trade exchange is the most appealing to manufacturers who want to move inventory but don't want to rely on either future cash outlays or limited avenues for fulfillment.

Not all full service corporate trades are like this. When the inventory is large, the spend-down has to be limited to one or two large cash purchases, such as media or travel. In these cases, full service exchanges will negotiate cash blends for the spend-down of their trade credits and generally perform exactly like corporate traders.

FULL SERVICE EXCHANGE DIVISIONS

Trade exchanges that offer full service divide themselves into divisions, each division with a specific task.

The job of dealing with excess inventory is commonly known throughout the industry as the AR (Asset Recovery) division. A variation of Asset Recovery deals with firms that cannot meet their obligations to financial institutions. In many cases, a business loan has been collateralized with inventory, and when this type of loan gets into trouble, the financial institution is forced to take possession of the inventory and try to dispose of it, usually for pennies on the dollar. It's an uncomfortable situation all around. The financial institution has to put out time and effort to get back a fraction of its loan through a liquidator, and the defaulting firm gets a black mark against its credit record.

The barter industry's response is to have a trade exchange take over the inventory of the distressed firm in exchange for paying off the financial institution in trade credits. The concept may be simple, but to be successful the trade exchange must have a solid client base to back it up and a good network for disposing of the inventory.

It's a win-win-win situation. The institution gains by getting its investment back in full purchasing power of product and services from the exchange; the defaulting firm escapes the stigma of bankruptcy; and the trade exchange has found another outside product it can buy with its trade credits. As with Asset Recovery, the inventory taken over by the trade exchange is usually sold either within the exchange itself or within its national network of affinity traders.

CREATING THEIR OWN MARKET

How can trade exchanges find markets for products so easily? The answer lies in the nature of the barter market, which is basically independent of the market-

place of America. Today's open market is suffering because of a shortage of money. The experts may argue as
to why the shortage is there; some say it's because too
many Americans are hoarding cash in socks under their
beds, others say it's because the government has soaked
up all the money available, and others claim it's the fault
of the Federal Reserve. At street level, it really doesn't
matter who's right or wrong because the problem for the
domestic marketplace is still lack of consumer buying
power, not consumer demand. The barter industry, by
creating its own purchasing unit, the trade credit, ensures that there's always plenty of "money" in the system
for those who want to carry on trading. Whether it's
uniquely styled plastic bottles or jewelry, a market need
can usually be found if the money is there for it.

A MONEY SUPPLY CREATES MARKETS

An example of demand following money comes from
Barter Network Inc., which has recently attempted to
broaden the base of its own full service exchange. Clients
can now negotiate loans of trade credits that are repaid
with products. For instance, a leather manufacturer
recently negotiated an expansion loan of $T25,000 that
was to be repaid in leather jackets, "sold" to B.N.I. at
wholesale prices. The only difference is that the prices
are in trade credits, not cash dollars. It's a deal similar to
an international "buy back" program in which an overseas investment in a manufacturing plant is repaid in
product rather than cash.

Ray Bastarache of B.N.I. has no problems with
accepting a hundred high-quality leather jackets as
repayment of the loan because he knows there is an
eager market among his clients, a market that doesn't

suffer from a lack of purchasing power. The manufacturer can use his loan of trade credits to expand his operations without taking out a cash loan that would have to be repaid for sales in an open, highly competitive marketplace. By pre-selling his product, he's removed any headache about repayments and is not reducing his credit-worthiness with an outstanding loan. It's a win-win situation that's made possible because Bastarache knows that "the marketplace will always respond to good product or service, providing the purchasing power is available."

PRODUCT SEARCH

Product search is a variation on the Trade Purchase Request developed by Sue Groenwald of Chicago Barter Corp. (C.B.C.). It grew right out of the tight money times of today and illustrates perfectly that the market is always there, even if the money isn't.

It works like this. Sometimes a client of the exchange will ask for a specific item, usually a large luxury item, that can't be found within the exchange's network. The exchange will then find that item in the outside market and negotiate a swap for credits. For example, an exchange member might want a Cessna four-seater airplane. Doug Dagenais of C.B.C. offers to locate the plane in the general marketplace and negotiate with the owner to sell it to the client for trade credits rather than cash. The owner can then spend the credits within C.B.C. The client gets his plane and Dagenais gets a commission.

This service is being introduced into the industry by several other commercial trade exchanges that are expanding their operations to become full service.

THE DONATED GOODS EXCHANGE

The search for new ways to use barter has led some exchanges to look at helping charitable institutions with donations. A manufacturer donates product or service to a charity. The exchange uses trade credits to buy the donated goods from the charity at manufacturer's cost. The manufacturer gets a tax receipt and a nice feeling. The charity gets the credits to spend within the exchange system and the exchange takes possession of the donated product.

Dagenais explains the philosophy and principle behind C.B.C.'s donated goods operations: "Many firms are far more willing to donate goods rather than cash to charitable organizations. The problem is that a lot of the donated goods have no relevance to that particular organization. What we do is provide a clearinghouse by taking in donated goods that an organization can't use and offering them a choice from our inventory. The donating firm gets a tax receipt and the organization gets product it needs."

For this service, C.B.C. charges an industry standard fee of 5 percent of the donated goods. Dagenais believes goods donations to be the most underutilized possibility in the industry, and he chides fund raisers for not making the most of the potential.

"Fund raisers tend to be stuck, like so many others, in the cash mode. If it's not foldable, it's not worth their time. But these days a lot of businesses are only too happy to donate their goods or services to a charitable cause. If fund raisers could only get into the idea that a charitable organization can meet a lot of its expenses through trade instead of cash, we'd all benefit."

*   *   *

Up until now, the full service trade exchange hasn't been able to deal effectively with the super-large transactions that are the hallmark of the corporate barter companies. Disposing of large inventories often requires a domestic or international network that has close connections with discount houses and other bargain retail outlets. Some corporate traders move their inventory through mail order outlets or particularly skillful negotiating. This type of big market savvy isn't accumulated overnight, but by moving into Asset Recovery, commercial trade exchanges have possibly taken the first competitive step that could easily grow into a direct raid on the territory.

The possible future of the full service exchange was summed up by an owner who wishes to stay anonymous:

"There are very few major trade exchanges that don't harbor expansionist plans. We'd all like to be a respected part of the mainstream marketplace, and that's only accomplished by expanding to a point where you can't be ignored. I see the growth of the commercial trade exchange to be limited by one thing only: good personnel. As we continue to attract more and more high-caliber people into the industry, anything could happen."

8

Countertrade

Back in the early 1970s the American public was treated to some bizarre newspaper headlines:

FROZEN FISH FOR BICYCLES IN CHINA—UK DEAL

U.S. MANUFACTURER TO SWAP DIESEL ENGINES
FOR POLISH JAM

What we were reading about were the first stirrings of countertrade: international swap and barter. It was a move that originated in cash-strapped Third World countries like Indonesia and Bangladesh, which decided that if America was going to sell to them, then America should buy from them. Within a few years, one hundred countries made countertrade a part of their official or unofficial government policy. American exporters suddenly found they were expected to take most, if not all, of their payment in products rather than cash.

American industry and government were furious at

this apparent betrayal of the free trade system. Other developed countries, particularly Japan, Europe, Korea, and Singapore, were more philosophical and went along with the changing marketplace. They cut deals with Borneo, taking exotic hardwoods as payment for cars and trucks. Britain swapped bicycles for China's frozen fish, and New Zealand shipped pedigree sheep and cattle to Iran in return for oil.

It was an idea whose time had come and it was impossible to stop. Countertrade today accounts for possibly 30 percent of the world's trading volume and continues to grow. Every day corporations at home and abroad make barter deals with one another involving billions of dollars of products and services. However, unlike the homegrown trade exchange industry in which it leads the world, the United States lags far behind in the use of countertrade. Precise figures are closely guarded, but estimates are that, by the year 2000, $1 trillion annual trade will be done through international barter and other cashless transactions. Unfortunately at present levels of involvement, less than 20 percent will be done by U.S. industry.

Dan West is executive director of the American Countertrade Association headquartered in St. Louis, a mutual support organization of 250 large and medium-size manufacturers, including GM, Boeing, and AT&T, which use countertrade as a part of their export strategy. West refuses to speculate on the size of countertrade deals within the association except to say they run from "about $100,000 to over a billion." He believes U.S. industry's response has been lukewarm to what he describes as "the competitive edge in a tough market."

"U.S. industry has to shake the belief that the world is still dependent on its products. We've got to face the fact that there is tough, aggressive competition out there, eager to cut our markets from under us, and counter-trade is a major tool for doing just that. As a nation, we would increase our exports dramatically if only industry would pay more attention to what today's market is demanding. In fact, I could see a more enthusiastic acceptance of countertrade leading a dynamic recovery in the American economy."

West is not the only countertrader who believes barter could lead the country out of its present economic slump. Jay Marshall is the president of Commerce Exchange, an international trading group based in Albany, New York. Marshall cut his countertrade teeth in the early 1970s as a facilitator in a ground-breaking transaction between Russia and PepsiCo. Russia traded PepsiCo the rights to market Pepsi for the exclusive North American distributorship of Stolichnaya vodka. Twenty years later this is still quoted as countertrade at its best. Marshall says it's no accident that the high-growth countries of Japan, Korea, and Singapore are also leaders in countertrade.

"When countertrade started to replace finance-driven trade, America lost ground because of a slow start. But we can still catch up if we recognize that the rules have altered and adapt to them."

The new rules are easy to understand: foreign importers are demanding a more level playing field on which more attention is paid to their needs as customers. They are saying, help us find the cash for what we do have and we'll be happy to deal with you.

It's a message with benefits on both sides. The U.S. International Trade Commission reported in 1985 that American companies engaged in countertrade had generally maintained or increased plant production and employment. Among the reported benefits were new business, larger and more efficient production runs, lower unit costs, increased capital formation, and the development of new technology to meet a more global demand.

COUNTERTRADE: BACKGROUND

Countertrade first appeared during the mid-1970s, when it was regarded in the same light as an open bribe. It seemed inconceivable that the preeminent position of the dollar in trade was being challenged. Appalled senators blustered about preserving the free markets of the world; economists were scathing on the claim that countertrade was a genuine market strategy. The idea that international swapping was of equivalent value to a deal financed through the International Monetary Fund (IMF) was outrageous.

The challenge continued, however, mainly because Third World countries had no other option. Their traditional means of trading had been yanked from under them and they were desperate for alternatives. The roots of countertrade are almost identical to those of contemporary barter. Just as a diminishing money supply has given a boost to national barter as an alternative money source, the changes in international banking policy have forced many countries to develop countertrade as an import policy. According to World Bank sources, commercial banks now lend only 5 percent of long-term financing to Third World countries as compared to 40 percent only ten years ago. The results have been devastating. Most LDCs—Less Developed Countries—need to import just about everything, from ballpoint pens to trucks to road-building and hospital equipment, all paid for in the currency of the exporting country. Without continued financing to pay for these imports, the entire socioeconomic of the LDC's faced chaos.

Until the dramatic changes in international banking policy, import financing was usually obtained through long-term loans from hard currency banks. But a series of repayment crises, touched off by Brazil, led to those sources drying up. For many LDCs, already scarcely able to meet interest payments on existing loans, it was imperative to find a way of getting vital imports without further draining their stock of overseas funds. Their solution was to implement countertrade: each import had to be matched by an equivalent value export of local product. "You can't sell to us unless we can sell to you."

At first it was a clumsy affair, with 90 percent of the deals collapsing under the weight of red tape, inefficiency, and downright fraud. Players in the early days of countertrade needed to be industrial giants, able to survive the losses, the lawsuits, and the aggravation. Lesser spirits would have given up, but the more far-sighted and aggressive stayed on to make it work. Their interest was far more than the sale, which often cost as much to put together as it produced in profits, it was that an LDC had something more valuable to offer than an order of trucks: in the long term, LDCs were potential markets of the future. By bending to countertrade demands, industries found they could get a foot in the door ahead of their slower and less sympathetic competition. By listening to LDCs and their needs, corporations were discovering a new, powerful tool not only for marketing but also for opening up new markets.

Doug Dagenais of Chicago Barter Corp. sees barter as a tool for incremental marketing. The concept is that by helping a client deal with his/her own inventory you can get a privileged trading position. Japanese corporations in particular were quick to spot the applications of this concept in their international dealings and set up remarketing divisions to help LDCs find markets for their products. As an example, Mitsubishi might sell an order of trucks to Borneo and be repaid in exotic woods. The remarketing division of Mitsubishi would find a hard currency market for the wood, sometimes in Japan itself, often before the transaction actually went through. It is an extra step in the business of export, but one thing is sure: Mitsubishi has a strong foothold in a country that one day will buy a lot of trucks.

An American pioneer in countertrade that played as much to the future as the present is McDonnell Douglas Helicopters. Back in 1984 the government of Hungary asked to purchase light helicopters for agricultural crop dusting. The snag was that the forint, Hungary's unit of currency, was regarded as worthless on the international money market. But an analysis of the situation showed that Hungary produced many things that could be sold in hard currency markets. Spark plugs, aluminum foil, and glass and steel containers were just some of the products that McDonnell Douglas Helicopters successfully remarketed in exchange for their sale. It was a turning point for the American giant, which now is probably the most high-profile of *Fortune* 500 companies having their own countertrade offices.

COUNTERTRADE: OPERATIONS

In earlier days, each exporter was expected to do his own remarketing. If you got paid in bamboo furniture for your delivery of oil drums, you had to find the market for them. Nowadays, that's not necessary. Countertrade has its own specialists, such as Dan West and Jay Marshall, who nurse the transactions from concept to when the dollars are finally deposited in the exporter's account. Dan West describes a typical contract with his firm, West Trade International:

"Supposing a manufacturer wants to sell fish boats to Indonesia. He may or may not have a buyer. If he doesn't, we'll first find a buyer and negotiate with the Indonesian government as to an acceptable counter-trade. This could be anything from rice to exotic woods to printed cloth or spices. If the contract is for $2 million we may have to find a countertrade for the whole $2 million, or often we can settle for less. Maybe the final agreement will be for $500,000 in fish products and the remainder to be paid in U.S. dollars or some other hard currency.

"Then we find a hard currency buyer for the fish, or a buyer with intermediate currency that we can convert into dollars. We look after the paperwork and bring the money home. In brief, we provide the service for the smaller manufacturer that a countertrade department performs for an industry giant."

Dan West is no stranger to this type of intricate trading. His employer before he founded West Trade was the chemical giant Monsanto, where he headed the countertrade department doing precisely the same sort of negotiations.

M. Jay Marshall's background clearly demonstrates that countertrade is not a field for beginners. After graduating from Columbia University in 1960, Marshall traveled the world putting together trade transactions of all types. In 1971 he entered the business of "commerce without currency" when he opened his own trading firm, but he still continued to consult for companies such as Mobil Oil and Revlon.

In the meantime he found the time and energy to start a trade exchange for local barter, a corporate exchange, and finally Commerce Exchange International, Inc. In the past twenty-five years, his clients have included General Electric, Budget Car Rental, Nestle, Sheraton Inns, and Addison.

Marshall has a staff of thirty with a wide range of abilities, not the least of which is fluency in several foreign languages. It's difficult to pin down a typical countertrade transaction. Marshall might be helping recover a trade-related debt in a country that has blocked the transfer of currency, or in another transaction, Commerce Exchange International might assist $53 million trade of computers to Canada for paper and lodging and car rentals for employees of the computer company.

"We traded $53 million of computers for $13 million cash and the balance in needed services and products. Canada? Why not? It's not a Third World country, but it still likes to sell as much as it buys."

Many of Marshall's transactions are multifaceted, some including the payment in products or services, others concentrating on bringing home the dollars.

"Every contract is different," he says. "The main thing is to maximize the return for all players and that can include all cash, or a mix of cash and product."

Marshall's approach is probably best illustrated by a 1989 transaction in which a European perfume manufacturer wanted to find an outlet for its product in the United States. Commerce Exchange International arranged for a hotel chain to take the perfume as a guest courtesy item. In return, the chain gave accommodations that were bartered to executives of a petroleum firm, which in turn provided the resin for the perfume bottles.

Although the contract was worth several hundred thousand dollars, the only cash required was for Marshall's commission and other expenses. The net result was that the manufacturer got an entry into the American market and was able to offset some of its manufacturing costs with the resin for its bottles. The petroleum company got a new customer plus hotel space, the hotel gained a very appreciated guest amenity, and Marshall enhanced his reputation as a shrewd trader.

Marshall credits much of his success in complicated transactions to his background, both in industry and as a trade exchange operator. They say that learning to sail a small boat is the perfect way to learn how to sail a boat of any size. Similarly, Marshall believes that learning the intricacies of supplying a client's needs at a local level is an excellent way to start understanding what is needed in the international arena.

WIDER OPPORTUNITIES

The appearance of independent countertrade specialists such as West and Marshall has meant a dramatic widening of opportunities for smaller export firms. According to Dan West, smaller countertrade transactions in the $100,000 range have appeared in the past five years that can often be successfully piggybacked on larger contracts.

Servicing a wider field of players has also meant evolving new forms to meet changing market demands. Originally based on the idea of a simple swap, counter-trade techniques now include bartering services, debt paper, technology, and U.S. expertise in marketing and education besides product; it's also moved from simply enabling trade turnovers to financing capital projects and production sharing ventures.

Countertrade specialists have had to broaden the definition of what they are doing. Most see themselves as marketing specialists for both sides of the transaction:

helping the importing country find markets for its products while smoothing the path for the exporter, which has made countertrade more accessible and simpler for U.S. industry. When asked what a potential customer interested in export should do, the invariable reply was simply: "Pick up the phone."

NEGATIVISM OF INDUSTRY

So why isn't it all happening? Everything is in place for a multibillion dollar export boom for U.S. industry, but instead all we're seeing is plant closures and more layoffs. Insiders believe a lot of American industry's woes can be traced directly to their own board rooms. "Dinosaur vision" and "fat-catism" are two unflattering descriptions of management's attitude that are frequently heard among countertraders.

Michael Morrison has been observing and commenting on countertrade since 1983. His newsletter, *Countertrade Outlook*, goes out from his base in Fairfield Station, Virginia, to all parts of the world. He thinks that American countertrade is good in the "boutique" business—corporations that specialize in countertrading one item—but that it lags woefully behind in broader markets. "There are many corporate heads in America who've made the conscious decision not to go along with countertrade. They believe that it's a privilege to buy American, and when liquidity returns to the global market, buyers will flock back to their traditional suppliers. It's an interesting judgment call but could cost a lot."

Morrison thinks a lot of this attitude is generated by a distaste for learning new techniques. American business generally has dominated world trade for so long it has fallen into a mold of simply selling for dollars.

"Collectively, the Europeans, Japanese, and Koreans are looking for market share through countertrade, and they're getting it. U.S. industry's sole objective is to look good on the next quarterly profits."

Countertraders have some suggestions of their own as to how to break the mindset they believe is a ball and chain around industry's recovery. Among the more creative solutions is a suggestion to mail every American shareholder a description of the countertrade option.

Jay Marshall says: "We've got to break the cycle of everyone telling each other that trade is all about price. American quality is always desired, but there days you also have to listen to your customers and help with their needs. It's not much to ask that a Third World importer of $5 million worth of American machinery get the same attention as a customer at any department store."

Gary Pacific is membership chairman for the American Countertrade Association and is manager of countertrade for McDonnell Douglas Helicopters. He also manages excess inventory recovery for the aerospace giant through corporate barters within the United States. Regarding countertrade, Pacific is particularly blunt in his comments to American industry. In a 1992 address to the U.S. Senate Commerce Committee on Countertrade, he is quoted by *Barter News* as saying: "This new international business environment presents a challenge to American businesses. U.S. companies must either rise to this challenge by implementing countertrade in their marketing departments or concede the international market to their competitors. . . . It should be realized that Americans have no choice but to do so because of a constipated domestic economy and an increasingly aggressive international market."

GOVERNMENT AND COUNTERTRADE ATTITUDES

But for all their harsh words, countertraders are emphatic that the initiative doesn't rest only with industry. The government itself has been dragging its heels in a number of ways, which has put countertrade at a disadvantage. While other foreign governments have eagerly cooperated with their national business world to seize the competitive edge, the U.S. government is still reluctant to face the message of Gary Pacific and others: without countertrade initiatives, American business will have to face the reality of being beat out in international markets.

The reasons for official heel dragging can only be speculated upon, but there is a general concensus that the U.S. government is uncomfortable with any move that might upset the General Agreement on Tariffs and Trade and the International Monetary Fund. As champions of a managed global economy, it is for the U.S. hard to encourage simultaneously the free-for-all wheeling and dealing that epitomizes countertrade.

The government is particularly wary of any move to use barter to escape established taxes and tariffs. Jay Marshall of Commerce Exchange International emphasizes that countertrade should never be regarded as other than a legitimate business option.

"I discourage any company from thinking in terms of evasion, either of taxes or tariffs. Countertrade is a viable marketing tool that shouldn't be tainted with shady practices."

Although he actually is an international countertrade consultant for certain major manufacturing states, Marshall doesn't draw back from attacking what he sees as a dilatory attitude within the federal government.

In one of his Commerce Exchange International papers called "Panic, Politics, and Countertrade," Jay Marshall sums up what he sees as the root of the U.S. government's fear of change: "Many superpower nations, the U.S. not least among them, established their power through the buying power of their money. Their dollars made them strong and the weakness of other currency served to increase their strength. A resurgence of countertrade threatens to shift that balance and undermine this strength.

"It puts the ball not into a new court, but within the realm of a whole new game. . . ."

Dan West puts equal blame on government economic advisors, saying they are presenting decision makers with a distorted vision of present world trade realities.

"Our economists were brought up to believe that everything finds its own level. If there's a scarcity in Uganda and a glut in France, they'll even themselves out—somehow. Somehow Uganda will find the francs or the dollars necessary to stay alive and functioning. With that type of philosophy, there's no need to find alternative methods of trade; you just keep waving your product and shout, "Over here." It takes a pretty rigid mindset to believe that's really what's happening in the world."

However slow the change, and for whatever reasons, countertrade is making itself known to American government. In December 1988 an interagency group, the Barter and Countertrade Division, was established by the U.S. Department of Commerce specifically for developing policies on countertrade and to study its impact on the U.S. economy. The agency draws on heavy hitters, including Defense, Commerce, Treasury, Labor, and Agriculture. The chief architect was Senator James Exon, who wrote that he hoped the new agency would give the

U.S. Government "a chance to turn its past dogmatic opposition to barter and countertrade into an opportunity to expand trade and create new markets for American products." In addition, the same executive order established an office of barter to handle questions from the public.

After five years of operation, detractors still accuse the agency of paying lip service to its mandate, a charge that is denied by Pila Vezariu, director of the agency. He makes a careful distinction between government-mandated countertrade and private transactions, stating that the U.S. government is only concerned with ensuring that contracts do not contravene the GATT (General Agreement on Tariffs and Trade, signed by one hundred countries). It may be a strictly correct position, but it hardly signifies the type of enthusiasm for which countertraders could hope.

POSSIBLE INITIATIVES

Government can help. Countertraders have no difficulty reeling off a list of things that would make countertrade easier both for themselves and corporate America. First, a generally more proactive stance by affected agencies would be welcome. Second, practical steps such as data collection, support for countertrade insurance, and a willingness for embassies and trade commissions to go after contract breakers in a foreign country.

"Generally, we want to see government support overseas trade deals as it does financial investments. Today, if a bank gets stuck with a bad overseas loan, the government will bail them out. But if a trader gets stuck, there's no one to turn to but the industry."

With the breakdown of the Soviet bloc there has been the emergence of a huge new trading market eager for American goods and technology. As China opens its doors, the possibilities for American industry have never been greater. But paradoxically it's in this period, when America has built its reputation to such a high, that it stands to lose all because of lack of flexibility, official and corporate.

It is a stance that has ruined the industrial bases of other countries that managed to become world leaders only to lose out to other, more limber competition. As late as the 1950s, British cars dominated the Canadian market but eventually were driven out as much by the take-it-or-leave-it attitude of British industry.

The question that corporate America must ask itself is, how badly does it want overseas markets? If the answer is positive, then corporate America must be prepared to use the techniques that are proving themselves right for the economic conditions of the nineties. Russia, or any other large market in the developing world, may want American-built, but if financing and servicing is available through countertrade with other countries, then it's obvious which way it will turn.

One countertrader has this to say about corporate attitudes: "Unlike domestic barter, which is unique to America, there is no need to speculate on whether countertrade is effective in the international marketplace. Indeed, a significant part of the reason why America is losing trading ground to Japan and Europe is their consistent and widespread use of countertrade in their dealings. There is absolutely no basis to the belief that American overseas trade is the victim of anything but its unwillingness to get involved with the new marketplace ethic."

9

UltraTrade: Star Wars Barter

The growth of barter within the United States has been explosive, but if a group of dedicated computer scientists, economists, and visionary businessmen has its way, the next explosion will be positively nuclear. In the fall 1993 *Barter News*, readers learned of a development that could possibly change forever the way in which corporate America does business. It is barter on a mammoth scale, so big that *Barter News* dubbed it "Star Wars Barter."

UltraTrade is the name for a barter program specifically designed to instantaneously find outlets for the underutilized productive capacity of American industry. It's done without trade credits, one-on-one negotiations, or the risk of nonfulfillment. By plugging into UltraTrade's ultrasophisticated computer network, a client can simply swap the product of his/her own excess capacity for needed products and services from other clients in the program.

For instance, a paper manufacturer with a $1 million

unused production capacity can place its own specific shopping list with UltraTrade. The program then searches the needs and products of all other clients until it has $1 million of needed products to swap for the paper manufacturer's excess production. Furthermore, the program not only finds products, it finds it at the best price, delivery date, and volume. As a safeguard for everyone involved, no deal is finalized until every client has given approval. At that time, a simple computer operation confirms all the trades involved, including delivery dates, shipping routes, taxes to be paid, and so on.

What makes UltraTrade so spectacular beyond the concept is the sheer scope and variety it offers. The heart of UltraTrade is an incredible computer program, eleven years in development at a total cost of $14 million, started by twelve experts in 1980, calling their company Advanced Artificial Intelligence Systems. The group has expanded to include twenty-six computer programmers, mathematicians, systems analysts, and business planners all focused on one problem: how to facilitate the intercorporate flow of goods and services and eliminate the need for an antiquated money system. Their solution was a computer program that could arrange complex barter swaps at lightning speed. It is this program which forms the base of UltraTrade.

On a daily basis, corporate America uses billions of dollars' worth of goods and services. Estimates of this interindustry flow is approximately $10.2 trillion annually, the value of the aggregate business done among the seven major components of the American economy. Although some barter of products and services does occur, most of this staggering figure must be financed either out of gross sales profits or through traditional borrowing.

The paper manufacturer, for instance, uses among

other things railroad facilities, chemicals, employee incentive plans and pensions, and protective clothing. To provide these things takes a bite of gross profits generated by sales. The manufacturer also needs office staff to deal with suppliers, process purchase orders, and generally keep on top of who's offering the best deal. On the other side, the railroad company, the employee pension fund, the protective clothing and chemicals suppliers are all faced with the same situation of meeting their ongoing needs out of gross profits and paying office staff to do the job.

UltraTrade's 16-gigaflop (16 billion calculations per second) program promises to eliminate most of this process for their clients through a series of instantaneous multiparty swap deals. The program will match one-on-one swaps (paper for chemicals), but it will also search for potential third, fourth, or even fiftieth party trades. Paper is swapped for paint, which is swapped for advertising, and so on until a final swap is made for the needed chemicals.

But availability of a product or service is not the only criteria for a successful trade. The program also sorts through all alternatives to find the best deal for overall cost. It even takes into account whether or not a proposed trade would be breaking U.S. antitrust guidelines, a significant consideration for the major players UltraTrade is hoping to attract. Finally, the program provides reports on transactions that come under the purview of the IRS's "Accounting for Non-Monetary Transactions." Because of the obvious barter nature of UltraTrade's transactions, clients are required to report on a separate IRS form 1099b.

Head offices for UltraTrade are with Advanced Artificial Intelligence Systems in Richardson, Texas. Actual research and development take place at a plant in California where the same group of scientists look for still faster ways of processing trade information. UltraTrade is a program that was created with maximum security as a major concern. Each of the computer programming teams was given a specific, isolated task to solve without reference to the overall picture. The result is that apart from a small team of coordinators, no one has an overall knowledge of the program itself. This is a particularly important point, not only for user security but also as a safeguard against industrial espionage. Future plans by UltraTrade go beyond the use of the program for massive corporate barter. The 20-dimensional matrix (artificial intelligence) system has many other applications in medicine, environmental strategies, biological, chemical, and pharmaceutical research to name but a few.

For the moment, however, the thrust of UltraTrade is on introducing a method of business interaction that could easily trigger a worldwide revolution, similar to that caused by the advent of the personal computer. James Cargile, vice president of administrative services, points out that the UltraTrade system is probably the largest commitment to the management of economic knowledge that has ever occurred and represents not simply a more detailed application of existing knowledge but an actual creative breakthrough.

"The UltraTrade program has the potential to put American industry into the forefront of world production by simply sidestepping the bottlenecks of an antiquated demand and supply system. The entire process of financing and stocking inventory and supplies is so cumbersome it actually slows down the efficiency of industry to a marked degree. We estimate that using a smoother system of exchange of product will actually generate billions for client users."

ULTRATRADE: BACKGROUND

With a potential for handling simultaneous trades for 400,000 corporations, the UltraTrade computer program is awe-inspiring. Development required breakthroughs in three major areas: data processing engineering, mathematics, and, of course, computer programming. The first step was to develop a model for the concept of simultaneous swap transactions.

Just one of the problems that faced the original twelve developers was designing a matrix that could handle all of the complicated calculations within a reasonable time period. The solution, the super-sparse matrix, was seven years in the making and took the program's maximum processing capacity from 200 to 12,000 client firms. In the next three years, researchers expanded that capability even further so that UltraTrade can now simultaneously mix and match the requirements of 400,000 client firms.

BENEFITS FOR CLIENTS

Cargile quotes several areas in which UltraTrade is expected to generate significant profits for the user company. For one thing, by ordering supplies on an as needed basis, storage costs, insurance, and security will be reduced. Also, the fact that financing will not be needed for UltraTrade purchases mean substantial savings in interest payments and the costs involved in getting such financing.

But like all barter transactions, the major advantage for the UltraTrade user is in the increased flow of goods and services that results from sidestepping present methods of sale and purchase. Just as a diminished money supply can cause an economy to grind to a halt, so the present necessity of third-party accounting and approval through the banking system means that instantaneous cash to make instantaneous deals is not always forthcoming.

UltraTrade places a lot of emphasis on the way in which purchases are instantly "paid for" by corresponding swaps of products and services. For example, a company looking to buy $5 million of needed goods and services will be able to sell the equivalent amount in excess production capacity in an instantaneous transaction—with nothing leaving anyone's plant or warehouse until everything has been balanced and approved.

TESTING POTENTIAL

Backing up Cargile's claims about dramatically increased profits is a test run in which 4,520 firms, all clients of "Big Six" accounting firms, were hypothetically run through UltraTrade's program. The results were impressive. According to Cargile, a typical major corporation increased sales by $115 million, while as a group, the 4,520 firms studied had an increase in gross profits of $110 billion.

Cargile comments, "Extrapolating these kinds of results over the spectrum of American industry means an almost instantaneous increase in interindustry flow of over $1 trillion—that's enough to trigger a revival in the American economy and keep us ahead in world trade for at least another ten years."

ULTRATRADE AND THE BARTER INDUSTRY

How does UltraTrade differ from the corporate trade exchange, which offers to take excess inventory in return for media time or other products? Significantly. One of the first differences that Cargile emphasizes is the guarantee of fulfillment. Since all deals through UltraTrade are preapproved, there is no more risk of nonfulfillment than in a prepaid business transaction. Indeed, since both parties are simultaneously both buyer and seller, even the hassle of collecting on the 30-day invoice is eliminated. Through the UltraTrade program there are no trade credits to spend down and none of the attendant worries about where to spend them.

Another obvious difference is the choice of products and services. A corporate trader usually offers discounted media or travel in exchange for distressed inventory. UltraTrade makes it possible for any corporation to swap identical values of inventory for any item that it wants for a simple 5 percent commission.

One final difference between UltraTrade and the corporate trade exchange is the final fate of the inventory. Under existing barter arrangements, a trading company that acquires inventory usually has to sell it to a cash market in order to recoup primary costs. UltraTrade operates differently. Inventory is swapped directly for needed products and services, all of which are used in the normal course of business.

CLIENTS

The procedure for any firm that becomes a client of UltraTrade is similar to that which McDonnell Douglas's

Gary Pacific proposed as a standard for corporate traders. First the client firm is analyzed for new potential
trades and sales. UltraTrade draws on business and
economic experts to help the firm decide just where and
how big these potentials may be. They also help draw up
a "shopping list" of the client's spot or ongoing needs to
be filled without a cash outlay.

UltraTrade then enters these parameters into the
program and decides on a market strategy relative to
other trades possible within the system, at the most
competitive price. Lastly, with all the buy and sell agreements in place, and all parties in agreement, the transactions are made by a computer command. From then
on, it's simply a matter of shipping and receiving. No
cash is involved.

Cargile emphasizes that UltraTrade functions strictly
as a clearinghouse for the transactions, and guarantees of
delivery or quality are the same as for any prepaid invoice.
He believes that intense screenings of potential clients will
ensure a high level of business ethics.

ULTRATRADE: POTENTIAL SNAGS

UltraTrade sounds like a greased wheels operation
and probably will be once the bugs are ironed out, but as
usual with most technological breakthroughs, the bugs
are not in the system so much as in gaining acceptance.
In UltraTrade's case, the threat to personal turf is considerable. Purchasing, accounting, dispatch, production, marketing—there are few areas in a corporation
that wouldn't have to undergo a significant dislocation of
existing practices in order to accommodate UltraTrade's
new economic order.

And if successful in even a small part of its ambitious agenda, UltraTrade will probably have to face considerable opposition from existing financial establishments. An offer to cut industry's needs for financing by a trillion dollars is not likely to be greeted with joy by those who make their living providing such finances.

A potential third difficulty to marketplace acceptance is still that old bugaboo, fulfillment. While UltraTrade may extol the virtues of instantaneous deals, it may find that manufacturers have a difficult time shipping high-quality goods on trust. A buyer of rusty widgets can threaten to withhold payment until they're replaced; a barterer could find it more difficult to get back his truckload of top quality paint, which has already been distributed throughout the system.

It's concerns like this—protective inertia, possible establishment antagonism, and worries over fulfillment guarantees—that UltraTrade's management seeks answers for as it heads for its critical mass of clients. Cargile claims that 31 specific major companies using the program would put UltraTrade on the map with interindustry trades that would instantly be greater than the entire existing barter industry. If the company clients were more random, it could take between 75 to 200 before the required diversity is reached.

In its drive to recruit clients, UltraTrade offers a free test run for any interested firm. Basically the same steps are taken as if the firm was an actual client: investigation of needs, a plan of possible fulfillment, plus a bottom line demonstration of potential profits. Cargile is naturally secretive about present client involvement but believes that at present levels of interest, UltraTrade will be solidly established and operational in the marketplace by the mid-1990s.

Ultimately, the success of UltraTrade may depend

not so much on the diligence of its sales force or the sophistication of its program but on how determined corporate America is to turn around its collective fortunes. UltraTrade, like countertrade and the domestic barter industry, is merely a marketplace tool specifically developed to deal with a stagnant economy. But the mere existence of these tools cannot inspire a corporate head to make use of their potential. That, like all business decisions, is a personal matter.

10

Starting an Exchange

More and more the barter industry is attracting the serious entrepreneur looking for unlimited potential in a fascinating field. What is actually necessary to start an exchange of your own? What does it cost, and what sort of commitment does it need?

THE MECHANICS AND THE COSTS

The commercial trade exchange is really the only type of barter system suitable for the start-up business. Countertrade and corporate trade require a level of expertise and understanding that can only be acquired through experience. On the other hand, a commercial trade exchange can be successfully operated by anyone with the enthusiasm, sales skills, and capital.

The physical setup of the simplest commercial trade exchange is not much different than an accountant's office or that of a stockbroker. As a bare minimum you'll need a computer and the skills to operate a fairly complicated database. You'll also need printed information, a phone, and a place to talk with prospective clients.

And then there's the money: you should preferably have enough to last you through a year of door knocking. A general consensus for those who have been there seems to say that a line of credit of at least $50,000 is the minimum needed for a start-up. Others say a more realistic figure is $150,000. Since a lot of early success depends on image and credibility, larger initial investments tend to produce faster returns. For instance, although many of today's major exchanges trace their roots to spare bedrooms or dusty cubicles in half-empty office buildings, it obviously helps if you can at least have a sign on the door, a carpet on the floor, and perhaps a secretary with a British accent.

TRAINING

Luckily some things have gotten less expensive with the passage of time. So much help and advice is available from the industry that no one has the excuse that he or she lacked knowledge of the nuts and bolts of operating a trade exchange. It's simply a matter of contacting the industry, saying you're interested in buying into an exchange or starting one, and asking what to do next. Invariably you'll be directed to one of the commercial trade exchange courses, which are found across the country.

An example is a training course offered by American Trade Exchange in Euclid, Ohio. This is a three-day program that combines a practical hands-on view of a trade exchange with classroom subjects such as sales and marketing, barter benefits, start-up procedures, computer requirements, and legal implications.

Enrollment for training courses and simple information is increasing rapidly as queries are coming from farther afield. Ray Bastarache of B.N.I. recently hosted a Japanese entrepreneur who is planning to open a network in Tokyo, and Terry Neale, president of ITEX, has opened offices in Australia and New Zealand.

Broker networks provide their own training and help in the initial setup of offices.

A smart move is definitely to join either IRTA or NATE and, if you're in California, maybe the California Reciprocal Trade Association as well. It's a matter of personal choice and philosophy which one you go with, but either way the rewards of membership are substantial. You'll be mixing with established exchange operators who have a lot of experience under their collective belt; they'll share it, too. NATE is especially proud of the seminars it runs regularly for trade brokers, on how to service and attract clients more easily. IRTA members spend a lot of time discussing management techniques and new wrinkles in the barter business. It all adds up to good value for a membership dollar.

PERSONAL COMMITMENT

Are you suited to owning an exchange? It's a hard question to answer because of the peculiar blend of skills needed. Starting an exchange from scratch or rebuilding one that has fallen into disrepair needs drive and entrepreneurial talents. Keeping an exchange alive and vibrant is another matter requiring strong managerial skills.

The personal commitment necessary is formidable, especially if you're aiming for the top. The industry has a plethora of stories of hard-driving men and women scrabbling their way out of basement suites into million dollar offices by dint of sixteen-hour workdays and undying vision. Unfortunately, if you don't have money to invest immediately in staff and premises, this seems to be about the only winning formula. Top operators such as Mike Ames, Ray Bastarache, Steven White, and Mark Tracy all paint the same early-days picture of skeptical friends, cramped quarters, and a feeling of fly or crash.

Most successful trade exchange operators have a background in some sort of hard selling. Starting the business is always the same: days of cold calling trying to sell something as nebulous as an idea that needs two-hundred people to make it work. Many successful owners confess to early feelings of panic when they walked in to the offices of their first customers and said, "I want to tell you about a barter system which I'm setting up."

ASSESSMENT

You do have to provide your own vision, but it can be sharpened by a detailed analysis of your potential trading area and by drawing up a sample client directory. It is said that Conrad Hilton spent his entire youth visualizing all the problems involved in owning a hotel chain, long before he was even old enough to have a drink in one. It's the type of mental exercise that *Barter News* recommends, and many exchange operators claim it is the cornerstone of their success.

Dreaming about barter, reading about barter, thinking about barter and how to make it work for you is probably a guarantee of success. After all, success in the barter industry, as in all things, must come according to how well you define it and how badly you want it. Only you can do that.

STARTING A TRADE EXCHANGE

There are three ways to establish a trade exchange:

1. Buy an existing one
2. Start an exchange from scratch
3. Buy a franchise or a broker's office from an existing network

The plan of action you choose depends on a number of things, including how much money you have, your commitment, and the scale at which you want to operate.

Buying an Existing Exchange

An exchange already in operation gives access to an established base and routine. It's an appealing course of action. The catch, as in buying any established business, is that if it's for sale the business is often one in trouble. Sometimes the problems are minor and can be repaired; lack of interest by the owner, for instance, is not lethal to future growth. Under new management and with new direction an exchange can quickly recover from simple neglect. What is more lethal are many, many dissatisfied clients or a bad reputation among businesses in the trading area.

Care is obviously needed when buying an existing exchange. The seller has the advantage of being able to paint whatever picture seems most appealing and, as in any business deal, an inexperienced buyer will rarely be able to pinpoint the trouble spots. However, exchanges do come on the market that require only a boost from fresh management to turn a ho-hum operation into a dynamic money machine. At the right price, buying an existing exchange can provide at least a minimal base of clients, hardware, software, and printing.

Trade Masters of Louisville, in Kentucky, is a good example of how to buy an existing exchange. In the spring of 1992 Carol Hutchison persuaded her husband that a local trade exchange would be a good investment. Carol already knew something of the barter business—her sister is part owner of Trade Masters of Atlanta, an organization that is building a broker network throughout the Southeast. But Carol didn't want to become a broker working for her sister; she wanted to be an independent, so she negotiated the right to use the Trade Masters name, bought the exchange, and set about building a clientele.

Although small, her new acquisition wasn't in the distressed category. It already had a solid base of 240 active clients, but there was obviously room for expansion. Within a year, Carol had brought in a full-time broker, office staff, including her daughter who is an accountant, and had signed on another 150 clients.

The Hutchinsons have their sights set on becoming a full service exchange dealing in corporate as well as commercial trade, but they are willing to put in the time building a solid retail exchange to back them up. Carol is an enthusiastic IRTA member and believes, like so many others, that the barter industry has barely scratched the surface of its potential.

"We both know that all we have to be is patient and thorough and the hard work will pay off."

Their break even point for the exchange came in the summer of 1993. They also augment income from the exchange with sales from a small showroom where clients can leave goods on consignment, and by moving small lots of distressed inventory.

"It's all good practice," said Carol, good humoredly. "They say moving $1,000,000 worth of inventory is no different than $1,000 worth. It's just a matter of zeros."

Starting from Scratch

Steven White started his Cascade Trading Association in Seattle in 1983. White caught the barter bug when he successfully traded construction work for the refinishing of an antique table. His first office was 200 square feet and his entire first year's trading volume was $30,000—profit, $3,000.

Growth was achieved through cold calling businesses and soliciting their membership and delivering on his promises. Today, White's exchange is the largest in the Pacific Northwest, and its trading is varied to say the least. His smallest transaction was 50 cents for a packet of Tums when a client decided to test the validity of his trade card at a local pharmacy; his largest trade so far was for a $60,000 real estate transaction. Being flexible to all needs is part of his ethic of "servicing his clients," obviously a winning formula. Of the first 50 businesses to join *Cascade,* 20 are still clients. In ten years White has powered up to a comfortable 700 client base and confidently expects to double his volume by the year 2000. Part of his confidence is based on opening another office in Portland, Oregon, and possibly another in Vancouver.

Unlike some commercial trade exchanges, White is not interested in expanding into the corporate trading field. Instead, he prefers to concentrate on attracting "storefront" clients, products and services found on Main Street, U.S.A. One way he has found of attracting more clients has been through offering even more products and services through an informal network of four other affinity exchanges with which he has developed a working rapport. Together the network forms a client base of about 2,500.

This development focus of a strong local base and affinity networking was also the direction chosen by Mark Tracy of Toluca Lake, California. When Tracy founded the American Commerce Exchange in 1981 he had only his selling skills and a gut feeling that the barter industry was the place for him. Luckily he was able to draw on the experience of Mike Ames, founder of TradeAmericanCard, the largest exchange in California.

"Mike has always been generous with his time and advice," says Tracy. "We've still got a strong friendship and cooperate with each other a lot."

With an active membership of around 500, American Commerce Exchange is a long way from such industry giants as Illinois Trade, which has almost 4,000, but Tracy has found that affinity networking is the perfect way to expand the trading horizons of his clients.

"We belong to a kind of unofficial network of other exchanges that we feel offer the same quality of service as ourselves. For instance, our clients can tap in any time to Chicago's Art of Barter or Illinois Trade. There's Barter-max in Boston, Systeme Truc in Quebec, Bay Area Barter in San Francisco, American Trade Exchange in Cleveland—these are just some of them. Obviously none of my clients are going to go to Quebec to get their car fixed with Systeme Truc, but they may well use us to bring in car parts from American Trade Exchange in Cleveland."

Tracy is convinced that the next leap forward in the barter industry will come through technology. He is already lining up for next year's Marketfax, a fax-based network for affinity traders, and is investing in new computer technology to give his office multistation capability.

"The less cumbersome barter is to use, the more clients will be attracted to it. Technology makes it possible for smaller exchanges to talk on an equal footing with the big ones, and makes us more appealing in what we can provide."

Like Steven White, Tracy has no plans to expand into the corporate barter field. "It's a whole new area of skills and contacts that I'm too busy to learn right now. Of course, if someone with a lot of experience were to come in and say they wanted to set up a corporate trade division for me, that would be a different story."

Unlike the larger exchanges, which prefer new clients to be requested from inside the exchange, White and Tracy still actively recruit from the business community at large. Tracy says, "Obviously we're sensitive to maintaining a good mix and not overcrowding a particular field, but we're not big enough yet to wait for the business to come to us."

Starting a Broker Network

The third way of owning an exchange is by buying a franchise or brokerage from an existing network. They will provide you with detailed training and 24-hour backup. You won't be totally independent, but you're not starting from scratch and you can run your own office and make your own mistakes. Buying into a network is simple and gives instant access to a huge variety of products and services.

It may sound high flying and impracticable, but given enough capital and drive it's also possible to create a broker network of your own, from scratch. If successful, the rewards can be substantial. What with broker's fees, transaction fees, and a huge membership to absorb inventory, a broker network can be a bonanza for the parent company. But starting one doesn't come cheap. Just the expenses of traveling around the country recruiting brokers can quickly run into hundreds of thousands. Estimates are that opening an exchange that plans to expand through a broker network could cost on the order of $1 million.

It is a formidable outlay, but there are broker network owners who started off exactly like this. Matt O'Hayer, president and CEO of Austin's Barter Exchange Inc., represents this new type of high-powered investment in the barter industry. O'Hayer was just twenty-six when he first came across barter as a business. He was impressed enough to put $100,000 on his own money into a start-up operation. Within eight months, his fledgling exchange was so successful that he raised an additional $1 million from a Philadelphia group of investors for a minority share in the company. Then he gave half back, figuring that he didn't want to part with so much control.

In ten years, this native of Rhode Island has built that $500,000 investment into one of the largest barter exchanges in the country. He did it first through franchising and then switched to establishing broker offices across the country.

Under O'Hayer's direction, Barter Exchange, Inc. grew fast, so fast that the prestigious business magazine *Inc.* named it as one of the 500 fastest-growing U.S. firms in 1988, and by 1993 it had a client base of nearly 7,000 from New York to New Mexico.

O'Hayer sees the spotty development inherent in broker networks as a necessary part of overall growth, which reflects broker enthusiasm more than faults within the system. His personal view of the future is optimistic, regardless of which way the economy moves.

"I think the best guess anyone can make about the world's economy over the next ten years is that it's going to be different. I have no problem with that. Barter was developed as a business survival tool, and even though it's grown from there, it still has its roots in hard times. Our attitude is that when the economy is good, barter's good. When the economy is poor, barter's better. It may sound flip, but it's true."

Barter Exchange Expenses

Running expenses for a barter system are high, particularly in the accounting division, which has to keep track not only of transactions but also satisfy the I.R.S. O'Hayer is typical of the new breed of barterers who combine meticulous attention to professionalism and ethics with the spirit of entrepreneurship. From the very beginning of operations, he insisted that Barter Exchange Inc. be audited annually by Peat Marwick, one of the Big Six accounting firms. Why?

"Professionalism, credibility, and knowing the bottom line," says O'Hayer. "By using a Big Six firm for annual auditing, you've already distanced yourself from a lot of yesteryear's problems."

Credibility is especially important to O'Hayer, who is actively planning to expand into Europe.

"There's a $5 trillion market over there being serviced by a Mom and Pop retail industry. It's a situation where the only thing that can hold us back is lack of adequately trained and motivated personnel."

THE COMMON CAUSE TRADE EXCHANGE

Stirrings of interest in trade exchanges are also coming from a quite different direction than the entrepreneur. Common cause groups, such as church groups, sports clubs, environmental groups, ethnic clubs, and business clubs, can benefit from establishing their own trade exchange. The advantages are obvious and immediate: an established group already has a critical mass of potential traders right within its own membership, which eliminates the need for time-consuming and costly initial growth.

One recent feasibility study for an international church group showed a potential for over 3,000 suitable clients with small- to mid-size businesses—perfect for an instant, vibrant trade exchange. What is even more perfect is that they already share a common faith, are interacting on a regular basis, and have built a level of mutual trust.

Tentative, and conservative, estimates show a potential income to this particular church group of about $1.5 million a year from transaction fees. The benefits to the members of having their own trade exchange are the same as for any other client: increased business and decreased cash flow for everyday expenses. Church leaders have also expressed the belief that trading would be a bonding for the members involved and provide a new base for reaching out into the community.

BUSINESS-BASED TRADE EXCHANGES

Yet another approach to getting a foothold in the barter industry is when an established business decides to open its own barter division. Circle Fine Arts, a publicly held group of art galleries with headquarters in Chicago, produces its own artwork through a network of international artists, which it uses to stock forty galleries throughout the United States. The company has grown over a period of thirty years to a point where it now has over 400,000 pieces of artwork worth over $200 million in working inventory.

Putting together such a collection requires a lot of products and services, and in 1982, president Ron Szekeres decided to investigate barter as a possible source. Today Circle Fine Arts sells about $3 million in artwork to over thirty different trade exchanges for trade credits. The trade credits are used to access products and services such as printing, quality paper, frame supplies, and packaging. Management is so keen on barter that a standing policy is that the accounts department cannot issue a check for cash without proving they have investigated a possible trade alternative.

"With such a background in barter it was a natural step to establish our own trade exchange, Art of Barter," says John Hora, director of marketing. "As regular clients of trade exchanges for the past ten years, we felt we could offer a high-quality exchange with a unique perspective on client problems and needs."

Established in April 1992, Art of Barter managed to bring in over 600 clients in its first year of operation. As enticements it has a lower transaction fee than most (4 percent on buyer and seller), no monthly service charges, and access to a huge informal network built by Ron Szekeres during his ten years trading.

"The network is vital," says Hora. "Everything stands or falls on trust in this business, and Ron has more than paid his dues. As a brand new trade exchange, we could find it tough going in a city that has so many large exchanges already established. But we also have the credibility and resources of Circle Fine Arts behind us, and that helps us make deals for our clients as good as the best."

Hora claims that the barter industry is in competition not with itself but with the cash dollar. He says that exchanges should concentrate more of their energy on helping people break away from a cash-dependent mentality.

"Trade is the mirror image of the cash economy. Cash is hard to get and easy to spend. Trade credits are easy to get, but you have to work at spending them. You have to research what you can buy, sometimes you have to decide what you can substitute for your first choice. Trade exchanges have to realize that cash is their greatest competitor. The way we can compete with cash is through better service, low fees, squeaky clean reputations, and throwing out the hustler image whenever it pops up. But mainly we have to make it as easy for people to use barter as it is to use cash. That's our greatest competitor, not another exchange down the road."

BUILDING A MEMBERSHIP

Establishing a strong exchange is a matter of bringing together the perfect clients. Just ten years ago, a trade exchange membership was likely to be composed solely of small business operators trading an average of $3,000 to $20,000 a year, but that has changed. The search for the perfect mix of clients is moving trade exchanges from simply accepting any application to a rigorous analysis of how well the new client will fit into the overall picture. While some networks are still open to new clients, others are opting for clients who will be aggressive traders and of maximum benefit to the system.

Typical of the new attitude is Steve Goldbloom's Bay Area Barter Exchange. Goldbloom's business philosophy has made the San Francisco–based exchange one of the most difficult—"exclusive," he would say—to join. When his exchange was featured on national television, he was swamped with hundreds of would-be clients, but he finally signed up less than forty. Why?

"I put most of my energies into increasing the sales volume of my existing clients," Goldbloom explained. "An exchange is about volume, not numbers in a client directory. A high volume shows participating clients who are happy with what's available and the services being offered. As a result of my particular focus, I believe Bay Area Barter has the largest trade volume/client ratio in the nation."

Goldbloom has seen his exchange flourish in good times as well as bad and disagrees with the idea that a bad economy is good for barter: "All a bad economy does is open people up to the concept of barter. But we do well in any economy, because there is always spare time and product out there to be moved. We enable that to happen."

At the end of 1993, Goldbloom had approximately 650 clients on his list—about 70 in Hawaii and the rest in the San Francisco Bay Area. He believes the Hawaii link to be of major importance in the success of the exchange. Hawaii members provide continuous, high-quality accommodations and services in a prime destination that he offers across the nation through reciprocal exchanges.

Chicago Barter Corp. President Susan Groenwald backs Goldbloom in his selective approach toward new clients: "We've had to say to people, barter just isn't for you. Originally we'd take in anyone who'd care to sign up, but experience soon showed that this was the wrong thing to do. An unsuitable client, one who doesn't approach trade and barter with some degree of enthusiasm, is bad for the entire system. He doesn't trade with members except as a last resort, he's always looking for ways to get cash rather than accept credits, and frankly, he doesn't produce any transaction fees for us."

Recruitment Methods

Recruitment methods have changed to suit the evolving picture. In the days before seminars and inter-exchange communication and training programs, how to recruit clients was a technique that was learned on the job. Any get-together of old-time traders is filled with wry laughter and anecdotes about the mistakes that were made and hard lessons learned. Today there's little argument that the key to good recruitment is always to set up win-win-win situations for the prospective client, his/her possible clients in the exchange, and the exchange itself.

Doug Dagenais of C.B.C. describes how he painfully learned this approach back in 1981 when Sue Groenwald, then the brand-new owner of a Barter Systems International franchise, recruited him as her first broker to bring in clients.

"Our client list was equivalent to my experience in barter—zero." he says. "It was tough. When a prospect would ask who else was in the system, I had to say, 'You're it.' Not many people signed on to trade with themselves!"

Dagenais soon learned that talking in rounded terms about trade exchanges just wasn't going anywhere. "People always want to know what's in it for them. They're not interested in a lecture about the future and what may happen. Talking about the potential of a barter network in Chicago did nothing for them. Their big question was always what was in it for them, *right now*."

Like any good rep, Dagenais changed his pitch. Instead of talking about potential markets, he learned to ask clients just one question: "What do you *want*?" If the answer was paper cups or snowmobiles or anything in between, Dagenais would go out to call on manufacturers of paper cups or snowmobiles, saying: "I've found another market for your product. Are you interested? And what do *you want*?"

"I felt like a juggler trying to get all plates spinning at once, and often I'd go back to a possible contact only to find the owner had lost interest or something else had cropped up." But eventually Dagenais started to get clients trading among themselves for the products and services they'd already asked Dagenais to find. It was an arduous way of building a client base, but looking back Dagenais insists it was, and still is, the only way to build genuine stability and long-term goals into the organization. By that year's end, Chicago Barter had 200 clients and had traded $800,000. It was a start.

In 1983 Groenwald terminated her contract with B.S.I. to start the Chicago Barter Corporation. Today the company operates out of a 9,000-square-foot office in Lombard, Illinois, with twenty-eight employees and branch offices in Milwaukee and Cleveland. Together they generate a cumulative trade volume of $20 million plus. C.B.C.'s client base is well over 2,500; a mixture of manufacturers, professionals, and retail business. Dagenais, now vice president, is still vigorously looking for new and creative ways of using the resources of the trade exchange.

Client Qualifications

Asked about his idea of the key to a successful exchange, Doug Dagenais emphasizes "diversity and activity." It's a belief that's common throughout the industry—the ideal client base must provide both. To get this ideal base, many large exchanges have developed tough specifications for their ideal client. They won't take on someone who won't benefit from barter or who won't be an asset to the exchange. They need to know that the prospective client will be able to trade his/her product or service. Are the products needed? Are the services sought after? A surefire way of knowing the answers is when those services or products have been asked for by a client already within the exchange. In fact, for some major exchanges, cold calling on businesses has become a thing of the past. They prefer to have the need expressed by the exchange clients before they go on a recruiting campaign.

For instance, a trade exchange client manufacturer may ask his/her broker to find a source of pallets that can be obtained through trade. If there is no suitable source within the exchange, the broker will locate an outside pallet manufacturer and try to recruit him. As a major selling point the broker will probably point out to the manufacturer that a trade sale is already set up and waiting—*a sale that would not normally occur through the regular marketplace.* It's a powerful incentive, very effective, and most large exchanges build their client base in this manner.

As a further incentive, the broker will ask the pallet manufacturer if there is a product or service that the exchange could provide for him. For instance, if the broker can find a source of pallet wood within the trade exchange, the manufacturer has an immediate place to spend down his trade credits on something he needs. It's a win-win-win situation: the manufacturer finds a trade source of pallets, the pallet manufacturer gains a new customer and is able to save cash by buying his wood with trade credits, and the exchange gains a new client and ongoing transaction fees.

The same dynamics apply if a new client walks in off the street and wants to join the exchange. He/she will probably be asking, "What do you want in services or products that the exchange can provide for you?" Insisting that the new client has at least some sort of shopping list within the exchange ensures that he/she will be an active trader and not someone just looking to unload excess inventory.

The potential client's service or product will also be assessed in relationship to the needs of the exchange as a whole. Of particular concern will be possible conflict through increased competition. The more sophisticated exchanges have developed a statistical research approach that tells them when certain products or services have reached a saturation point and bringing in more will be counterproductive.

With these new recruitment procedures there already seems a danger that some larger traders won't be promoting barter among small business anymore. It's an unfortunate trend that can only be countered by men like White and Tracy, who still believe in building from Main Street U.S.A. Without mid-size exchanges like Cascade Trading Association and American Commerce Exchange, small business America could be in danger of being passed over in favor of the high-rolling, more aggressive traders and the entire industry could become an exclusive domain.

Client Maintenance

A lot of the profit for the trade exchange is through transaction fees, which is one reason why operators focus on increasing their volume of trade. If a client is trading $4,000 a year, most exchanges will focus a lot of effort on raising it to $6,000 or $8,000, or even more if possible. They do it by frequent client contact through their brokers, asking such questions as what they have for barter and what they need, particularly drawing their attention to new barter opportunities.

Apart from raising the income from transaction fees, another reason for focusing on encouraging the clients to keep trading is the specter of network failure, even for the largest operations.

Building a membership into a critical mass is one thing, maintaining and expanding it is another. Without adequate income from transaction fees, some trade exchanges have lost their growth impetus and have been stuck for years—some since the early 1980s—with a membership of a hundred or so, never quite getting big enough to generate their own dynamics. Others simply collapse from lack of interest and participation by the members.

Most people presently using barter systems are aggressive consumers, determined to get what they want through unorthodox channels if necessary. But if not, Matt O'Hayer of Austin's Barter Exchange Inc. offers this advice to the new exchange owner: "A significant number of barter systems fail to survive into a second year of operation and even fewer into the fifth. They fail for a number of unique reasons, one of which is that members simply stop using them—they collapse because the clients have become consumer wimps. A barter system is like a bicycle—you have to keep pedaling and putting out energy if you don't want to fall off."

For O'Hayer, pedaling means member involvement. If enough members stop trading, the entire system grinds to a halt. The trade exchange doesn't get its transaction fees and is forced to close its doors.

There are any number of reasons why members stop participating, but the single, most damaging trend that a trade exchange owner must face is when members don't fully grasp the difference between barter and money systems.

"Barter members need to adopt a different attitude toward trade credits than the one they have toward regular dollars," O'Hayer says. "It's pointless saving trade dollars except for a specific purchase—in fact, it's better if you don't. Trade dollars are for spending and any trade exchange operates best when everyone wants to consume even more than they want to sell."

Keeping that attitude alive and well within the system is the most critical activity of any network owner.

NETWORKING

Any new or small-size trade exchange is attracted by the concept of networking, formally or informally. Networking to increase product availability, either through a formal broker or an informal cluster of affinity traders, is a concept that just won't go away. However, a new or very small exchange rarely has the product base to attract the attention of an affinity trader. If someone is going to deal with you, then they will obviously require that you have as much to offer them as they can offer you. Therefore most networks that attract the new or small independent exchange are those set up formally as an umbrella network, overseeing and facilitating trades.

Every year or two another such network springs up

with much fanfare and then usually quietly dies away. The concept of a formal national or regional network of trade exchanges is similar to the broker network. Member trade exchanges are brought together under one central office that acts as a clearinghouse and monitor for the system. Commercial trade exchanges that join networks agree to take one another's trade credits at par and treat one another's clients as their own. The appeal to small exchanges is that by tapping into a network that already exists, it should be possible to provide a much wider selection of products and services and generate more transactions among clients.

For the ambitious operator who has bought a small exchange, affiliating with an established national or even regional network can be a good move. A network can provide immediate assistance to the new exchange and be a shortcut to larger inventory and a larger client base. But it's not all as simple as it sounds, and there are some things to watch out for. Formal intercity networks have run into rough waters in the past, primarily over different values of trade credits among the member exchanges. Items tend to vary wildly in price from exchange to exchange, and exorbitant cash blends are sometimes demanded. Other complaints are poor delivery of products and even inferior products to what has been promised. It is all so often a case of "out of sight, out of mind" and can make for unhappy clients.

A decision to join in intercity trading needs to be approached with more caution than enthusiasm. There are some critical questions you need to ask. First, can you access the entire product and services of other member exchanges, or are you simply offered access on a time-to-time basis? Second, are the products and services of another exchange priced at the same level as your own? Third, can you freely contact other exchanges for their experiences to date?

If you can't get satisfactory answers, then maybe the best thing for you to do is build up your own network of affinity traders. It may take longer and it needs a lot more work, but the results for both you and your clients will make it all worthwhile.

SUMMARY

If you can think accounting and selling at the same time, there are many doors into the barter business. If you belong to the management of a common cause organization, you've probably got all the major components in place for your own trade exchange: a valuable service to the members and a source of revenue for headquarters. If you have the money and the opportunity, you may want to cut down on start-up time by buying an existing exchange. A speedy way to build up a client base may be through accessing more products through intercity trading, formally or informally. Or you may just want to buy a franchise or a broker's license from an established network.

Whichever way you go the one sure thing is that the field is still open for anyone who wants to try. The barter industry needs new ideas and skills as much as it needs new clients, and the rewards can be substantial for anyone who can grab a vision and build for the future.

11

Legalities and Establishment Reaction

But how legal is all this? It is possible to simply set up your own money system and start making loans from it to the public? It could be argued that trade dollars are actually a micro-money system within the larger money system created by the Federal Reserve. Certainly trade dollars have all the characteristics of a viable currency. Indeed, with an estimated $30 billion in products and services to back them up, the total trade credits in America's barter industry represent a greater buying power than the GNP of many countries.

Today, the issue of the nation's money supply is legally the sole right of the Federal Reserve banks. Other banks also need official registration in order to function, but only the conglomerate of banks known as the Federal Reserve are permitted to create money for the nation's use. It must be assumed, therefore, that barter systems fall into the same area as the early banks that printed their own currency and loaned it to the public. It was all perfectly legal but not all that well regulated.

THE INTERNATIONAL RECIPROCAL TRADE ASSOCIATION (IRTA)

Insiders agree that the original pioneer of the present-day barter industry was Marvin "Mac" McConnell, who in 1960 sold his Inglewood Thrift and Loan to start the Executive Exchange Club, a recognizable forerunner of the modern trade exchange. But it wasn't until 1969 that McConnell had worked out the bugs sufficiently to start franchising his operation. By then it had become Barter Exchange (BX) International, a state-of-the-art trade exchange that set a high ethical example for the burgeoning barter industry.

Ironically it was McConnell's success that nearly killed the industry before it even got started. Many franchisers who imitated McConnell quickly realized that the shortest way to wealth was not to follow McConnell's formula of careful customer service and a rigid code of ethics but deficit spending.

Lack of regulations allowed such problems to go unchecked, and insiders soon realized that the industry would have difficulty establishing a solid growth pattern until it established some sort of official structure.

Attempts at professionalism within the industry began in 1979 when McConnell joined forces with other concerned exchange operators to found the International Reciprocal Trade Association (IRTA). The aims of IRTA were simple but high minded: raise the barter industry from its free-for-all status to a sober, responsible profession. The only member of the association who was not a barter exchange operator was Paul Suplizio, the executive director. His firm, Suplizio and Associates, specialized in political lobbying and was soon called upon to prove its value.

The fledgling group set out to get other operators' cooperation to draw up a code of ethics and standards of compliance. It was a sorely needed step, but one that was not met with much enthusiasm by the majority of barter operators. They were operating in a virtually unregulated field, and many were dazzled by the potential for quick profit.

Even some members of IRTA were not exempt from the feeding frenzy of the time. The founding members soon found themselves and their ideals swamped by an influx of operators who wanted to use the association to move barter even further away from any type of official legislation. A particularly bitter fight developed over IRTA's decision to try for official recognition of the trade dollar. Proponents believed that the barter industry needed this recognition to move forward and establish itself as a bona fide industry. Opponents wanted to keep the freewheeling status quo. One pressure group even wanted the trade credit to be declared officially valueless as a means to avoid paying income tax. McConnell fought vigorously against the move, but after only two years left IRTA convinced that it was heading for the rocks.

NATIONAL ASSOCIATION OF TRADE EXCHANGES (NATE)

A splinter group, which accused IRTA of deserting the original ideals of the association, left to found their own National Association of Trade Exchanges (NATE).

In some ways it has been a split that has benefited the barter industry since it provided two organizations, each encompassing different philosophies. IRTA members tend to be high rollers with a heavy focus on corporate trade and the big ticket trades of distressed inventory, lease traps, and media time. NATE members tend to be commercial trade exchanges with sights set on solid growth within their own geographic area. Between them, the two organizations manage to provide support for just about every type of operator and operation in the industry, something that could be quite difficult for just one association to do.

Dual memberships are not common, and each association talks of expanding its own memberships instead of amalgamation with the other. As is usual in this type of situation, both organizations claim the high moral ground, and although NATE does have more stringent rules for membership, it's all a big question mark as to who has the most white hats in the hallway.

When it comes to gaining official recognition, each organization typically takes opposing views. IRTA tends toward pushing the federal government for self-policing powers and often likens the present barter industry to the early days of unregulated securities sales. To curb the wilder elements within the industry, Suplizio favors self-regulation, presumably with IRTA doing the policing and enforcement. NATE, on the other hand, favors a more neutral stance.

However, so far the government has expressed little interest in the views of either group. In spite of significant recruitment efforts, no effective champion has come forward to submit a bill that will give the industry the teeth it needs to regulate its own members. The improvements that have occurred in the industry so far have been brought about by peer pressure and the triumph of good business sense. Another significant factor in curbing the excesses of yesteryear has been the IRS involvement in the industry.

THE INTERNAL REVENUE SERVICE AND
THE BARTER INDUSTRY

During the early 1980s internal dissent was not the only problem facing the barter industry. The Internal Revenue Service had decided that barter exchanges were hiding places for tax dodgers, so they conducted a vigorous campaign to prove it. In the space of a few months they issued over two-thousand random John Doe audit summonses against barter exchange members. A John Doe summons meant the audit could be on any exchange member, and the word soon spread to the public that joining a trade exchange was a certain ticket to a tax audit.

It was a public relations disaster and IRTA moved against it with all the resources at its disposal. Luckily, the facts were on their side. After two-thousand audits the IRS admitted that exchange members were not only paying proper taxes but that there seemed to be less tax evasion than there was among the general public.

An unofficial interpretation of their final decision is that the act of bartering is no more illegal than making a simple purchase or working for wages. It's perfectly legal for you to paint a neighbor's fence in return for her Dodge pickup, and any government that believes in free enterprise should encourage such initiatives. However, in certain cases the law does require you to report the transaction for income tax purposes.

As a general guide, if you are exchanging services for which you normally get paid, then you must report the value of what you receive as income. For example, if you are a professional painter and you and your neighbor have established that the pickup is worth $300, then you should report an income of $300 for painting her fence. If the pickup is for business purposes, it should be reported as a capital investment. However, since your neighbor is not in the used car business and therefore doesn't make a regular profit from trading cars, then she does not have to report $300 for the "sale" of her truck.

However, this general guide doesn't apply if your neighbor's truck is actually registered as an asset of her company, in which case the fence painting done in exchange is registered as income. How much income? The IRS Code Section 1.61-2(d) (1) and (2) relies on "fair market value" to define how much the painting or the truck is worth. They even make an effort to describe what is considered fair market value—the price that would normally be expected in the open market for a service or product.

In theory, painting a fence for a truck could possibly be used as an example of a tax neutral transaction: both parties receive equal income and both have equal expenditures. However, the transactions still have to be reported to the IRS. You can't simply claim that no one made a profit and therefore you don't have to report.

Every year each barter exchange is required by law to report directly to the IRS every transaction that goes through its system. The clients also receive a record of their own transactions plus their account standing at year's end. This information is submitted to the IRS on an official tax form. For the calculation of tax, all trade credits are taxable for the year in which they are earned, not spent.

It was this ruling by the IRS plus a U.S. Tax Court finding that deficit spending was income to the exchange owner that effectively capped the spate of deficit spending that had plagued the industry since its beginnings.

LIKE-KIND EXCHANGES

Barter may not be used to avoid the payment of tax but certain types of barter have the advantage of tax deferral. Section 1031 of the Internal Revenue Code allows for tax deferral in *like-kind* transactions for real estate and business equipment. For instance, a printer who exchanges one type of print machine for another may only have to pay tax on a positive cash difference. It's an appealing side of barter but needs a competent tax counselor to sort out the ramifications.

THE TAX EQUITY AND FISCAL RESPONSIBILITY ACT

Project Barter, the name the IRS gave to its raid on barter exchange members badly shook the industry. To stop the situation from recurring the directors of IRTA decided they needed some sort of understanding with the tax authorities. On August 16, 1982, IRTA Executive Director Paul Suplizio called a strategy session of IRTA supporters and mapped out plans to help passage of TEFRA, the Tax Equity and Fiscal Responsibility Act. If passed, the act would provide the barter industry with its first official recognition as a legitimate industry.

The legislation introduced two important things. First it protected members against John Doe audits by recognizing barter exchanges as third-party record keepers. This put them on an equal footing with banks, credit card companies, securities brokers, and accountants. Second, TEFRA required barter companies to report the annual barter income of their members to the IRS on form 1099B.

On September 3, 1982, President Reagan signed TEFRA into law and the barter industry stood on a new threshold of development. IRTA looked forward to the day when the federal government would go one step further and give it self-regulatory powers to control abuses in the industry and take it one rung further up the ladder of respectability. The association formed BARTERPAC, Barter Political Action Committee, to accept in-kind contributions from trade exchanges to federal candidates.

But respectability wasn't that easily won; in fact, TEFRA probably gave a burst to the more lawless side of the barter business by providing some legitimacy. Deficit spending and wildcat franchise companies sprouted all over the continent. Between 1979 and 1983 there were more than 140 failures of barter systems in California alone, most due to deficit spending. The total value of products lost by California businesses to deficit spending in those four short years was estimated at between $70 and $100 million. No figures are available for the rest of the continent, but simple extrapolation shows a possible continent-wide loss of $1 billion—at a time when gas was 50 cents a gallon and the average family home cost $50,000.

In 1985, irate demands from California businesses that the state government do something about widespread rip-offs led to the introduction of AB 124, a bill that would have effectively killed the barter industry in California. The bill would have prohibited a trade exchange from buying or selling with its own trade credits, which would cut out deficit spending but also cripple the exchange's ability to operate.

At a tense meeting of IRTA and NATE in Burbank it

was realized that the passage of AB 124 could lead to a spate of similar legislation across the country, effectively closing down the entire industry. A massive national letter-writing campaign persuaded the California committee to tone down AB 124. It was reintroduced as AB 1529 and Suplizio was dispatched to Sacramento to press for its acceptance.

He did extremely well, speaking eloquently on behalf of the struggling industry, pointing out the groundwork for ethical conduct already established by IRTA and basically pleading for a stay of execution. On April 17 the new and milder bill, under the name California Barter Bill AB 3363, was accepted by the Assembly.

Although diluted, the bill laid down some strict rules of behavior. Barter operators in California would be registered and bonded with the State Department of Justice, annual financial statements would have to be produced, and it would be a misdemeanor for an exchange to deficit spend or spend unearned credits. Vague promises to prospective clients were no longer allowed, and a specific contract would have to be presented to them with all restrictions and rights clearly spelled out.

The bill was still seen as posing too big a threat to the industry, which claimed that increased paperwork alone would cost each exchange thousands a year. Another national letter-writing campaign was mounted, which resulted in the bill being scrapped altogether. Foremost in this countermove were the seven California trade exchanges that would have been most affected by the proposed legislation. They banded together and eventually became the California Reciprocal Trade Association with Mike Ames of TradeAmericanCard as president. Hyped as a trade organization on the outside, its essential purpose was the defeat of the negative legislation, which it accomplished. In 1987, CRTA was officially launched, but it failed to evolve into the network originally envisioned by Ames and others.

THE PRESENT

It would be nice to report that IRTA went on to more and greater legislative triumphs, but it didn't. Suplizio's cherished goal of a self-regulating industry is still a long way from reality and may even be fading. Opposition to such a move now comes from as much within the industry as out, some insiders saying that self-regulation carries too much danger of vested interest groups seizing control of the industry.

Mark Tracy, president of NATE, doesn't support regulation by either the industry or government. He points at the existing financial institutions that are heavily regulated yet still plagued by scandal and incompetence.

"We're in a business where people are finding out it's more profitable and more satisfying to build solidly and for the long haul. That's the fact that will eventually bring stability to the industry. If you put in too many arbitrary levers of control, you open up a political nightmare of who controls who, something which has always worked against free enterprise."

But many of IRTA's other goals are gradually being reached. Most of the association's activity is concentrated on building solidity in membership and reputation. Although only about 30 percent of the nation's approximately 400 trade and corporate exchanges belong to IRTA, they represent many of the top earners in their fields.

NATE is also working toward the similar goal of an

industry that regulates itself through enlightened self-interest. Regulation of ethical conduct may be coming about as a byproduct of competition rather than legislation. In a tortoise and hare scenario the exchanges that stuck to solid growth patterns have edged out most of the speculators in the field. The unscrupulous operator now trying to establish a foothold finds he has to compete against exchanges with a ten-year reputation of good client relationships and responsible accounting. This practical effect, plus vigorous public education by IRTA, NATE, and individual exchanges, is making it more and more difficult for the con artist to find a foothold in the industry.

12

Barter and the Marketplace: The Future

It's easy to see why barter systems flourish during economic hard times—it's the time when they're needed most. But there are other reasons why barter systems are moving from the fringes of Band-Aid solutions into our mainstream economic systems, even to the point of becoming the preferred method of trade for some people.

One reason is the perceived instability of the banking system is general. Barter members have told me time and again about their qualms about the banking system and their belief that the massive Savings and Loans collapse of 1990 was just the tip of the iceberg. This unease about the stability of the dollar and those who look after it is being translated into a new economic life-style, with barter systems at its core. The general theory is that a barter group is the epitome of a tightly knit group that could survive economic collapse.

Economic survivalists say the future of barter systems is closely tied to economic conditions. Although people will always prefer cash and the greater variety available in the open market, we may be moving into an era of unprecedented economic chaos in which case barter and barter systems could be the network that holds American business together.

It may never come to the worst case scenario, but there are clues that without heroic efforts to turn it around, the United States may be heading for substantial social dislocations in the near future. The social visionaries are already prophesying that the new America will have to contain a much greater percentage of self-employed; jobs now threatened or lost can never be replaced and Americans will have to relearn the self-sufficiency of yesteryear.

It's already a trend that is noticeable. Bryan Doyle, has lectured for twenty years on the development of small business, says that in the past two years there has been a dramatic and sustained increase in enrollment. "North America is getting the idea that we can no longer rely on heavy industry to provide lifetime security and work. People want to discover what working for themselves is all about; it's often the only alternative they have."

Barter flourishes in this type of environment, whether it's simply friends exchanging baby-sitting or free trucking in return for construction materials or a massive countertrade deal that will put a tomato plant in the Ukraine and take payment in canned tomatoes. As government attempts more and more ways of cutting expenditures, the privatization of the United States will continue at an accelerated rate, forcing many to develop entrepreneurial skills in every area.

Can our present financial system keep pace with these types of new development? Probably not. The money system has become a giant whirlpool in which new money is immediately siphoned off to pay old debts. To aggravate the situation, much new American money is being generated not for investment at home but for giant developments around the world. A case in point is the new marina at Mazatlan, Mexico. Billed as the largest in the world, the total construction cost is $800 million, most of it supposedly from the States.

The need for a significant alternative trading system is already becoming apparent. As has been said, the market will always respond to a good product if the money is available. The barter industry, as a whole by accident or design has already laid the groundwork for an alternative that could carry the United States through a difficult period of readjustment. The trade credit system is in fact almost a duplication of the dollar system and can be expanded just as easily. The real stumbling block for the barter industry as a whole is not will it work, but can the right people be found to answer the demand?

Problems with money supply aside, another theory as to why barter systems are so rapidly becoming mainstream is the supposed death of "mass consumerism." Some of the more advanced thought in today's marketplace says that present dislocations and shifts in the nation's economy indicate more than a few technical problems with money supply. The traditional marketplace is under attack not only from money deflation but, more significant in the long run, from changing societal values about consumerism and material greed. New perceptions by the buying public about the environment, mass commercialization, and the demand for more quality time are changing forever the way people shop and what they shop for. Even if good economic times return rapidly, the marketplace and particularly ways of selling and buying will probably never be the same again. The consumer society of tomorrow will be less status oriented, and more aggressive in its search for the best deal.

Pundits of social change say that even before the present depression, society was already turning away from the traditional marketplace and toward a more freewheeling, hard-nosed approach. Hard times have merely accelerated a process that first started to show with the environmental movement of the late 1970s. The consumer is becoming more aware of manipulative sell tactics and is rejecting them in favor of a more deliberate individual choice.

The traditional marketplace relied on impulse buying and often tried to goad the consumer with such devices as status and emotional gratification. As long as these types of motives were at work, it made sense for retailers to invest in exotic outlets such as the upscale mall and for the manufacturer to emphasize trivial differences in their products. The consumer of yesterday expected to be pampered and cajoled, and the way to do it was through lavish marketing, which translated into massive overheads. We all knew what was happening but few objected to paying prices that were grossly inflated by marketing and packaging. The important thing in the days of mass consumerism was the emotional satisfaction that went with the actual purchase itself.

But now marketing experts believe that society is going through a disenchantment with mass consumerism as a way of life and that this disenchantment won't change with an upturn in the economy. Everywhere they are seeing signs that the old Madison Avenue line of "sell the sizzle, not the steak" is not working as well as it used to. Even among the remaining shreds of the comfortable middle class, fewer and fewer people are "first price buyers." As a society, we're becoming more canny about what we buy and why we're buying it. We're rejecting the emotional high of the consumer marketplace with its loaded overheads and are opting for simple, no-frills transactions where we feel we are getting solid value. As one marketplace watcher observed, we are finding a joy in "consumer puritanism."

This trend bodes well for barter systems, which are more intimate, more personal, and in which the individual can usually find better bargaining and better results. For many aficionados, barter systems represent a return to simpler values and a way of life. They are the corner store in place of the supermarket, offering similar rewards and limitations. They may not provide the entire range of products and services, but they do give greater satisfaction in personal relationships and frequently better value for what is available.

These two trends—consumer puritanism and distrust of existing systems—are pushing people to align themselves with what they regard as a simpler life with better rewards, and barter is being identified as belonging to that life. It's doubtful if this redirection of societal focus is going to vanish with an upturn of the economy; in fact, most are prophesying that this demand for more substantial values will increase, taking barter systems along with it.

Many barterers love the fact that they don't have to part with cash and often talk about barter as eventually replacing the money system itself. It may never get to that point, but there's no denying that barter systems are helping many continue to work and make deals while bureaucrats scratch their heads and wonder what to do.

The eminent practicability of barter systems as an alternative money supply has got some industry leaders thinking about wider applications with far-reaching social implications. There has even been talk of customized barter systems to meet special situations, which have been happening in company towns devastated by closures and massive layoffs. A barter system run by the municipality could help everyone through the tough period of adjustment that lies ahead. Other new applications for barter include helping ethnic and other special interest groups establish their own systems, both for the profit of the organization and also for the members.

Barter is hearing the message and moving toward the challenges of the larger picture. Leaders in the industry, confident that they have left the early confusion behind them, are now making plans for national and international deals on a scale that were unimaginable just ten years ago. Barter system operators of today are looking to a future of vast networks of interlinked systems to provide a greater array of services and goods for individual members.

It's a plan of action and a vision that the United States should not ignore. In spite of political promises, there is no doubt that the marketplace has been pretty well abandoned by traditional investment to readjust to the new realities of world economics. That adjustment may take five years or fifty, but in the meantime there is no reason why Americans should not exercise their old passion for initiative, ingenuity, and entrepreneurship. Whether it is the band of geniuses who sweated for eleven years to develop UltraTrade or Shari Baker in Phoenix carefully posting the Barter Group's transactions, or Dan West trying to awaken American industry to the potential of countertrade, America has the people and the tools for survival. The big question now is: Has America lost its dream? As a nation, have we become so complacent with the way we do things that we can't adapt to new situations? Are the CEOs of American industry still motivated by a 10 percent increase in business or a 15 percent decrease in expenditures, or is the charge of fat-catism justified? Will small business owners be galvanized by the potential of saving their businesses by simply changing the way they operate?

Not so long ago, Americans raised their kids, built their houses, dreamed their dreams, and lived their lives using cash on the rarest of occasions. Then something happened and we lost our understanding of how to access things without money being involved. Well, the money isn't there now so the problem is how to get people to link their dreams with the concept of barter instead. When this attitude really takes root, it will mean barter systems are not only here for the hard times but as an active part of a new societal ethic.

APPENDIX A

National Association of Trade Exchanges (NATE): Membership List

1994 President
LES FRENCH
Alphanet, Inc.
9790 SW Pembrook St.
Portland, OR 97224

AMERICAN BARTER CO.
SANDRA DODSON
1326 Malabar Rd., Suite 6
Palm Bay, FL 32907

AMERICAN COMMERCE EXCHANGE
MARK TRACY
10556 Riverside Drive
Toluca Lake, CA 91602

AMERICAN NETWORK EXCHANGE
HAROLD RICE
912 E 63 Street, Suite 200
Kansas City, MO 64110

AMERICAN TRADE EXCHANGE INC.
TOM MCDOWELL
27801 Euclid Avenue
Euclid, OR 44132

ART OF BARTER INC.
RONALD SZEKERES
303 E Wacker Drive, Suite 830
Chicago, IL 60601

BARTER ADVANTAGE INC.
LOIS DALE
1751 2nd Avenue
New York, NY 10128

BARTER BUSINESS EXCHANGE
ROBIN MAINI
2777 Steeles Ave West, #202
Toronto, ONT 0043J

THE BARTER CONNECTION
SUSAN WILLIAMS
889 41 Avenue
Santa Cruz, CA 95062

BARTER CONNECTION INC.
JANE DARLING
38 Antares Dr., Suite 300
Nepean, ONT 00225

THE BARTER GROUP
SHARI BAKER
8700 East Via de Ventura,
#205
Scottsdale, AZ 85258

BARTER SYSTEMS—SAN ANTONIO
BOB MCLAREN
4254 Gatecrest
San Antonio, TX 78217

BARTERMAX
AL KAFKA
Box 415
Sharon, MA 02067

BAY AREA BARTER EXCHANGE INC.
STEVE GOLDBLOOM
582 Folsom St.
San Francisco, CA 84105

BXI—SOUTH GEORGIA INC.
FRANK SCOTT
1520 Pine Lodge Road, #3
Conyers, GA 30207

BXI—TULSA
ALAN ELIAS
4815 South Harvard, #510
Tulsa, OK 74135

BXI—WEST
ALAN ZIMMELMAN
600 So. Curson Ave., #319
Los Angeles, CA 90036

CASCADE TRADE ASSOCIATION, INC.
STEVEN WHITE
500 Wall Street, #417
Seattle, WA 98121

CONSUMER BARTER OF FLORIDA
THOMAS PARKER
11495 66 St. North
Largo, FL 34643

CONTINENTAL TRADE EXCHANGE
DON MARDEK
Box 51035
New Berlin, WI 53151

COOPERATIVE TRADE EXCHANGE
INC.
JERRY ARSENAULT
1717 20 Street, #106
Vero Beach, FL 32960

EXCHANGE ENTERPRISES
MICHAEL BUTWORTH
50 Washington St.
Norwalk, CT 06854

FINANCIAL INTERCHANGE GROUP
LESTER ABRAMS
RR 4 Box 200c
Atlantic, IO 50022

GULF COAST TRADE EXCHANGE
BOB CRUMPTON
2525 W. Fairfield Dr.
Pensacola, FL 32505

HEARTLAND BARTER EXCHANGE
ROY TUCKER
122 Main St.
Cedar Falls, IA 50613

ILLINOIS TRADE ASSOCIATION
JACK SCHACHT
4208 Commercial Way
Glenview, IL 60025

INTERNATIONAL BARTER EXCHANGE
RON UNGER
Box 20188
Sarasota, FL 34276

ISLAND TRADE CENTER INC.
SAM CASSARO
130 Mathews Drive
Hilton Head Island, SC
    29926

ITEX—NEW YORK
DONALD TROOIEN
115 West Jericho Turnpike
Huntington Station, NY
    11746

LEISURE CORP
ALAN WOLFSON
80 SW Eighth St.
Miami, FL 33130

THE M. E. NELSON CO., INC.
RONALD FRIEDMAN
16 W. 45 Street
New York, NY 10036

MEDIA TRADE EXCHANGE
JOHNNY EAGLE
6960 Lee Highway, #105
Chattanooga, TN 37421

MIDWEST BUSINESS EXCHANGE LTD.
JERRY HOWELL
5111 East ML Ave, #11B
Kalamazoo, MI 49001

MIDWEST TRADE EXCHANGE
GARRY MONKMAN
2300 Green Bay Road
North Chicago, IL 60064

NATIONAL COMMERCIAL EXCHANGE
RICHARD HARRIS
106 Four Seasons Center, #107
Chesterfield, MO 63107

New Orleans Trade Exchange
Cindy Braiwick
Box 15068
New Orleans, LA 70175

The Savannah Trade Exchange
Chip Burch
7505 Waters Road, B-10
Savannah, GA 31406

St. Louis Trade Exchange
Therese Launhardt
11420 Gravois Rd.
St. Louis, MO 63126

Summit Trade Exchange
Robert Boone
216 W. Superior St.
Duluth, MN 55802

System Troc Inc.
Parise Marcel
3333 Cavendish, #275
Montreal, Quebec 0054

Trade Exchange Inc.
Dean Hnilica
1546 Bourbon Parkway
Streamwood, IL 60107

Trade Network Inc.
Gary Kay
Box 700
Haslett, MI 48840

Trade Systems Interchange
Danny Weibling
5350 Commerce Blvd.,
    Suite C
Rohnert Park, CA 94928

TradeAmericanCard
Mike Ames
777 South Main, #77
Orange, CA 92668

TradeRight Inc.
Marl Quinn
45 Plant Road, #109
Hyannis, MA 02601

Unlimited Business Exchange
Ken Meharg
926 Eastern Ave.
Malden, MA 02148

APPENDIX B

International Reciprocal Trade Association (IRTA): North American Membership

Public Relations
Paul Suplizio
IRTA
6305 Hawaii Ct.
Alexandria, VA 22312

AAIS, Advanced Artificial
Intelligence Systems
JAMES C. CARGILE
397 Dal-Rich Village, #230
Richardson, TX 75080

Active International
ALAN S. ELKIN
1 Blue Hill Plaza, #520
Pearl River, NY 10965

Active International
ART WAGNER
1 Blue Hill Plaza, #520
Pearl River, NY 10965

Active Asset Recovery
AL HOLLAND
1 Blue Hill Plaza, #520
Pearl River, NY 10965

AlphaNet Inc.
LES FRENCH
9790 SW Pembrook Street
Portland, OR 97224

American Barter Co.
THOMAS SHIPMAN
467 Green Tree Road
Sewell, NJ 08080

American Trade Association
DAVID WALLACH
Box 285
San Rafael, CA 94915

Associated Corporate Barter
  Services
MATTHEW TALBERT
15477 Ventura Blvd., #300
Sherman Oaks, CA 91403

Baltimore Barter Connection
FRANK SCARPOLA SNR.
3615 Courtleigh Drive
Randallstown, MD 21133

BarCo Inc.
RICHARD HUNTER HOWARD
Box 522
Ridgeland, MS 39158

Barter Atlantic Ltd.
RALPH GASS
Box 2874
Dartmouth, Nova Scotia
  B2W 4Y2

Barter Card
RAY BROWN
822 Cumberland, #1
Little Rock, AR 72202

Barter Connections Inc.
KENNETH C. BARRON
822 Boyleston Street
Chestnut Hill, MA 02167

Barter Exchange Inc.
MATT O'HAYER
1120 Capital Texas Hwy.,
  S/Bldg. 3 #300
Austin, TX 78746

Barter Exchange of Eastern
  NM/Amarillo
TIM VALENTINE
225 Innsdale Terrace
Clovis, New Mexico 88101

Barter Exchange—Dallas
LARA SHAW
55 Arapaho Village
Richmond, TX 75080

Barter Exchange—Houston
GARY E. BELL
16431 Heatherdale
Houston, TX 77059

Barter Exchange—Midwest
MARK LINDEMAN
4537 N Shadeland
Indianapolis, IN 46260

Barter Exchange—Tri City
RONALD H. ESPOSITO
120 N 8th
Killeen, TX 76541

Barter Network Inc. (CT)
RAYMOND BASTARACHE
53 River Street
Milford, CT 06460

Barter Network Inc. (MA)
RAYMOND BASTARACHE
45 Plant Rd.
Hyannis, MA 02601

Barter Plus Inc.
JAMES HOOPER
1242 Whitfield Ave.
Sarasota, FL 34243

Barter World USA
JEOFFREY HORNER
4837 Foxshire Circle
Tampa, FL 33624

BarterPlus Systems Inc.
MICHAEL CARON
2 Lansing Square, #804
North York, ON M2J 4P8

Bay Area Barter Exchange Inc.
STEVE GOLDBLOOM
582 Folsom Street,
San Francisco, CA 94105

Bay Barter Co. of R.I.
ERIC GODFREY
564 Eddy Street, Box 2593
Providence, RI 02906

Boston Business Exchange
STEVE LICHTMAN
278 Mystic Ave., #207
Medford, MA 02155

Bureau Int'l D'Echange
YVAN ALLARD
2300, rue Leon Harmel
  Bureau, #110
Quebec, G1N 4L2

The Business Barter Group
TERRY MCCULLY
762 Upper James, #316
Hamilton, ONT L9C 3A2

Business Buyers Network
RALPH BUTTS
95 Main Street
Maynard, MA 01754

Business Trade Alliance
VINCENT SCHUETZ JR.
5960 Dearborn, #11
Mission, KS 66202

Buyers Business Network
FRANK O'DELL
95 Main Street
Maynard, MA 01754

Buyers Wholesale Company
CHARLES RALPH BUTTS
95 Main Street
Maynard, MA 01754

BX International Inc.
STEPHEN FRIEDLAND, President
245 East Olive, #200
Burbank, CA 91502

BXI—Arizona
TERRY BRANDFASS
6560 N. Scottsdale Rd.,
  # H-105
Scottsdale, AZ 85253

BXI—California
P. RONALD KEISTER
Box 2556
Carmel by the Sea, CA
  93921

BXI—Middle East Tennessee
PAMELA LEE DUZAK
305 Park Circle
Nashville, TN 37205

BXI—Sacramento
JUDY RADER
6728 Fair Oaks Blvd.
Carmichael, CA 95608

BXI—San Diego
DUNCAN BANNER
3200 Adams Avenue, Suite 205
San Diego, CA 92116

BXI—Southwest
THOMAS AUSTIN
Box 866454
Plano, TX 75086–6454

BXI—Ventura/Santa Barbara
DIANE M. VAN TREES
4732 D Telephone Road
Ventura, CA 93003

BXI—West
ALAN ZIMMELMAN
600 S. Curson Ave., Suite 319
Los Angeles, CA 90036

Chicago Barter
  Corp/Sourcecorp
SUE GROENWALD
800 E Roosevelt Rd.
Lombard, IL 60148

Chicago Trade Exchange
  Inc.
DEAN E. HNILILA
850 E. Higgins, #20B
Schaumburg, IL 60173

Cleveland Barter Corp.
WARREN OSTERGARD
29313 Clemens Rd.,
  Suite A
Westlake, OH 44145

Comtex Trade Exchange Inc.
HERBERT TEICHMANN
1000 De La Montagne
Montreal, Quebec H3G 1Y7

Cooperative Trade Exchange
  Inc.
GERALD ARSENAULT
1717 20 St., #108
Vero Beach, FL 32960

Corporate Investment Barter Ex.
JEFFREY BURKHARDT
1150 Berkshire Blvd.
Wyomissing, PA 19610

Creative Barter Network
GAILENE YATES
Box 338
Arnold, MD 21012

CSI International Inc.
JUNE BRODY
800 2 Avenue
New York, NY 10017

CSI International Inc.
WILLIAM SCHACHTER
800 2 Avenue
New York, NY 10017

Cushman and Wakefield
WILLIAM CONWAY
1410 17 Street, #200
Denver, CO 80207

Deerfield Communications
GERALD FINGERHUT
88 University Place
New York, NY 10003

Delaware Barter Corporation
RON WHITNEY
2500 W. 4th Street, #2
Wilmington, DE 19805

Energy Systems Financial Corporation
TED DEMMON
Two Lafayette Court
Greenwich, CT 06830

Euram
RICHARD VISSERS
253 Merritt Mall,
Suite 584
Merritt Island, FL 32952

The Exchange
SCOTT WHITMER
5072 Edgewater Drive
Orlando, FL 32810

The Exchange Connection
JAMES L. BLANKENSHIP
Box 1121
Bedford, VA 24523

Flying A Advertising
MICHAEL AMSBRY
51 Federal Street, #103
San Francisco, CA 94107

Font Business Exchange Inc.
JOEL C. FONT
8 Ivy Court
Clifton, NJ 07013

Global Exchange Network Inc.
SONDRA AMES
1920 Main Street,
   #200 Koll Center
Irvine N
Irvine, CA 92714

Global Marketing Resources
SHARON GERSON/DAVID
   ROSENAUER
551 Fifth Avenue
New York, NY 10176

The Herrington Corp.
CLYDE FABRETTI
2605 Hannah Farm Court
Oakton, VA 22124

Icon International Inc.
LANCE LUNDBERG
220 E. 42 Street, #1601
New York, NY 10017

Int'l Exchange Network Inc.
D. HARRISON
8550 Pie 1X Boulevard,
   #440
Montreal, Quebec H1Z 4G2

International Barter
   Exchange
RONALD D. UNGER
4000 S Tamiani Trail,
   #408
Sarasota, FL 34231

International Barter Group
DAN GERHOLD
2231 Technical Pkway.,
   Suite C
N. Charleston, SC 29418

International Barter Network
KEN YEOMANS
21 Gladstone Ave., #305
Oshawa, Ontario L1J 4E3

ITEX Corporation
MIKE BAER
Box 2309
Portland, OR 97208

ITEX Licensed Broker
DIANE DONNELLY
1050 Pipeline Road, #202
Hurst, TX 76053–5731

ITEX Licensed Broker
ARTHUR SEABORNE
8051 N. Trail, #44
Sarasota, FL 34243

ITEX Licensed Broker
BILL BALTAS
5135 Elm Ridge
Baton Rouge, LA 70817

ITEX Licensed Broker
J. UNDERWOOD
Box 470962
Charlotte, NC 28247

ITEX Licensed Broker
CAROLINE MILLER
1830 NW 23 Place
Portland, OR 97210

ITEX Licensed Broker
MARY SCHERR
Box 455
Glastonbury, CT 08033

ITEX Licensed Broker
CHRIS CHRISTENSEN
1834 N Parkway
South Belmar, NJ 07719

ITEX Licensed Broker
ELIZABETH SCHERR
7000 Broadway, Bldg. 1
  #106
Denver, CO 80221

ITEX Licensed Broker
RICK OWENS
800 118 Ave., NE, Suite F
Bellevue, WA 98005

ITEX Licensed Broker
KAREN HOFFMAN
11710 Administration Drive
St. Louis, MO 63146

ITEX Licensed Broker
BRUCE KAMM
Box 6849
New York, NY 10128

ITEX Licensed Broker
LAURIE DANCER
6516 North 7 Street, #1E
Phoenix, AZ 85014

ITEX Licensed Broker
PAUL MCCONVILLE
2855 Anthony Lane South,
  B-50
Minneapolis, MN 55418

ITEX Licensed Broker
BILL ZIMMERMAN
675 Delaware Avenue, #107
Buffalo, NY 14209

ITEX Licensed Broker
JULE GULLEY
2065 Peachtree Industrial
  Ct., #215
Atlanta, GA 30341–2244

ITEX Licensed Broker
D. CLARK
4040 Pala Mesa Oak Drive
Fallbrook, CA 92028

ITEX Licensed Broker
TODD DEWEESE
14347 SW Teal, #40
Beaverton, OR 97005

ITEX Licensed Broker
WALT MYRICK
3915 N Penn, #101E
Oklahoma City, OK 73112

ITEX Licensed Broker
MARTHA HEIMBUCH
Box 1554
Grand Island, NE 68802

ITEX Licensed Broker
LISA KOPPELMAN
10300 SW Greenburg Rd.,
   #370
Tigard, OR 97223

ITEX Licensed Broker
DAVID HELLER
3050 E Desert Inn,
   #116
Las Vegas, NV 89121

ITEX Long Island
DONALD TROOIEN
115 West Jericho Turnpike
Huntington Station, NY
   11746

The International Marketing
   Exchange
CARLO PARENTELA
7501 Keele Street,
   #303
Concord, ONT L4K 1Y2

The Intrac Group
JEFF MOHN
640 Fifth Avenue
New York, NY 10019

Jones and Jones
JUANITA JONES
138 Augusta International
Kiawah Island, SC 29455

Livinston Financial
DAN LANGTON
Box 6359
Incline Village, NV 89450

Media Barter Associates
HAROLD CUMMINGS
150 E 58 St.
New York, NY 10155

Media Exchange Inc.
BETTE BRYMAN
5505 Roswell Road, #350
Atlanta, GA 30342

Media Resources
   International
PETER BENASSI
275 Madison Avenue
New York, NY 10016

Media Resources
   International
RICHARD CHASE
310 Washington Blvd., #206
Marina Del Rey, CA 90292

Merchants Exchange
JANE GOEI
1480 Broadway
San Diego, CA 92101

Milt Warner Associates Inc.
ERWIN ROSNER
114 East 32 Street, #702
New York, NY 10016

Nambu International
PAUL DANIEL
712 Fifth Avenue
New York, NY 10019

National Commerce
  Exchange
RICHARD PAER
400 Jericho Turnpike
Jericho, NY 11753

NCE of Tampa Bay
BARBARA ARCHIBALD
12360 66 St.,
  Suite H
Largo, FL 34643

New York Barter Corp
DOROTHY ROGERS-BULLIS
Box 8463
Albany, NY 12208

Novus Marketing Inc.
DAMIAN TOPOUSIS
601 Lakeshore Parkway,
  Suite 900
Minneapolis, MN 55305

Reciprocal Marketing
  Sources
PERRY SILVER
225 West 34 Street
New York, NY 10122

Remax Realty Plus
SIROUS JAFARI
12321 Middlebrook Road,
  Suite 270
Germantown, MD 20874

Sterling Holdings
HEIDI OTTO
Box 1273
Millbrook, NY 12545

Thomas J. Conlon Inc.
THOMAS J. CONLON
Four Cedar Swamp
  Road
Glen Cove, NY 11542

Touch Talk Inc.
ROBERT DAY
1800 N. Meridian,
  Suite 401
Indianapolis, IN 46202

Trade Exchange of America
177 Clay St.
Muskegon, MI 49440-1212

Trade Exchange of America
RICHARD LINZELL
1408 S.W. 13 Court
Pompano Beach, FL 33069

Trade Exchange of America
7858 West Central
Toledo, OH 43617-1530

Trade Exchange of America
FRED DETWILER
23200 Coolidge Highway
Oak Park, MI 48237

The Trade Exchange Inc.
BILL AUSTIN
27 Gorham Road
Scarboro, ME 04074

Trade Masters of Louisville Inc.
PAUL HUTCHINSON
10311 Bluegrass Parkway
Louisville, KY 40399

Trade Masters of St. Louis
TERRI LAUNHARDT
11420 Gravois Rd., Box 270330
St. Louis, MO 63136

Trade Partners International
CYNTHIA PARKER
232 W Crogan St.
Lawrenceville, GA 30245

Trade Services International
LISA PETERS
1160 N. Dutton Ave., Suite 180
Santa Rosa, CA 95401

Trade U.S.A.
ROBERT WILBER
6301 Gaston Ave., Suite 500
Dallas, TX 75214

Trade Works Inc.
RICHARD HURLEY
187 Columbus Turnpike, Suite F
Florham Park, NJ 07932

TradeNet
JERRY ROBERTS
10926 Huston Street, Suite 204
North Hollywood, CA 91601

Tradewell West
HAROLD REED
388 Market St., #400
San Francisco, CA 94111

Tradewell Inc.
MIDGE TYNER
845 Third Ave.
New York, NY 10022

U.S. Commerce Exchange
JOHN PIMENTAL
1017 17 Street, Box 2781
Key West, FL 33041

United States Barter Group
RON WEPRIN
203 Rockway Ave.
Valley Stream, NY 11580

Valley Trade Exchange
DONALD FREEZE
205 E. Noble Ave.
Visalia, CA 93277

Vermont Barter Network Inc.
WILLIAM BURNETT
Box 746
Milton, VT 05468

Vista Media Inc.
MITCHELL SCHULTZ
3500 Victory Blvd., Suite
   A-421
Staten Island, NY 10314

NOTE: Only members of NATE and IRTA are listed here. For a complete list of exchanges belonging to broker networks, contact their respective head offices.

Index